Christian Bahr

Divided City
The Berlin Wall

Photos and Facts

Personal Accounts

Traces Today

Jaron Verlag

■ GREETING

from Klaus Wowereit, the mayor of Berlin

Today very little in the city recalls a structure that people throughout the world associate with the name Berlin. People who walk through the German capital today can hardly imagine how a wall could have divided this lively metropolis into two halves and how for over 28 years – from its construction on August 13, 1961 until it fell on November 9, 1989 – it divided a city into two worlds.

The 13th of August, 1961 made Berlin's difficult situation appear even more hopeless. The western part of the city was hermetically sealed off by GDR border troops.

All at once, close relatives, friends and acquaintances could only wave to each other from a distance. It was no longer possible for them to meet. Overnight the Wall tore families and friendships apart, it shattered hopes and destroyed life plans.

The day the Wall was built marks the beginning of a brutal border regime. Well over a hundred people lost their lives in a desperate attempt to overcome this wall. The Wall continued to cost lives and cause injuries because there were always people willing to attempt adventurous escapes in order to reach freedom and they often paid for their courage with their lives.

It took time to recover from the shock of the Wall being built and for the city to return to business as usual. Through the policy of small steps it was possible over time to at least make the Wall a bit more open. But even when people from all of Berlin were once again able to see each other in the eastern part, this did not diminish the tragic consequences of the division.

The international political situation in the 1980s created conditions that made it possible to overcome the division of Europe and hence also the partition of the city. The Iron Curtain was raised bit by bit, first in Poland and Hungary, where similar to the GDR, civil rights activists achieved political rights in a peaceful revolution.

The fall of the Wall on November 9, 1989 marked a climax in this international political process. The Wall disappeared overnight and with it, one of the sinister symbols of the Cold War.

In Berlin today, the impact of the division has not yet been overcome completely. Much has been achieved in recent years, but there is still a lot to do.

The remains of what was once the Wall will forever recall the unhappy period of division and remind us of the victims. They also urge the people of today not to forget the past and to overcome the consequences of the Wall.

INTRODUCTION

A not so normal train station in a not so normal city. Friedrichstrasse station, a heavily guarded border-crossing (1982)

Friedrichstrasse Station. "Everybody off. This train ends here!" A train station in Berlin. The end of the line for trains coming from opposite directions. Two separate train station halls, two different worlds, hermetically isolated from one another. The people pass by without seeing each other. Every move is kept under surveillance, observed by ubiquitous police officers, undercover secret service agents, hidden cameras. Friedrichstrasse Station – an eerie border-crossing.

What seems unimaginable today was routine in Berlin yesterday – in divided Berlin when there was only East and West – two incompatible systems, enemies, competing for victory over world history. A trench, created by mistrust and confrontation, cut through the German city in the center of Europe.

The twenty-eight years that Berlin was divided had an immense impact on the city, an impact that can still be felt today. The division is still present in the lives of the city residents, in the traces that the Wall left behind

on the cityscape and in the relationship between two different societies in the process of growing together. Berlin and the Wall are still inseparably intertwined. Even though the border ceased to exist on November 9, 1989 and on October 3, 1990 the once divided city was reunited and established as the German capital. Even though the people from the East and West by now live integrated daily lives together in the city. And even though the empty strips of land left behind by the border are slowly disappearing. The division continues to be an important part of Berlin's identity.

The residents may no longer be so aware of it, but for visitors and new arrivals to the city, Berlin's unique history still remains quite vivid.

In fact, the challenge of searching for and discovering the remains of the heavily guarded border area in the center of a European city continues to attract tourists from all over the world.

On August 13, 1961, life in the city changed dramatically. Suddenly watchtowers, border soldiers, escape attempts, deaths, separation from loved ones and the restriction of movement were a part of the daily life of the people who lived in Berlin. The Wall created a situation that is hardly fathomable – a situation which lends greater meaning to the word "freedom."

How did it happen? Although the Wall came unexpectedly, descending upon the city and its residents overnight, the plan to erect a barrier at the border had a long history. The division was caused by the formation of political power blocs in Europe after the Second World War. Two conflicting social systems had consolidated themselves on the continent: free democracy in the West and centralized Communism in the East. The military alliance against National Social-ist Germany had disintegrated. The United States, France and Great Britain were now on one side and the Soviet Union on the

Berlin was a scene of devastation following the defeat of Hitler Germany (1945)

other, and they competed for world supremacy. The emergence of an east-west conflict had major consequences for Germany, a nation that had been conquered and occupied by the four Allies. The country in the center of Europe formed the frontline of the Cold War. Each ally developed a different political and economic system in its own sector. In 1949, two separate states were founded: The Federal Republic of Germany (FRG) and the German Democratic Republic (GDR). Berlin was situated in the middle of the GDR.

War-damaged Berlin was, like the entire country, also divided into four sectors by the Allies in 1945. The former Reich capital was put under a special four-power status, which meant that the United States, Great Britain, France and the Soviet Union administrated the city together and with the same rights, with each ally maintaining jurisdiction over its own sector. Until 1948 the four allied commanders of the city worked more or less peaceably together. But then, in 1948, the first open confrontations broke out between the USSR and the western powers. The currency reform – the introduction of the West German D-Mark in the three western zones of occupations – provided Moscow with a reason

to cut off the connection between Berlin's western sectors and West Germany on June 24, 1948. The Soviets blockaded the western section of the city for eleven months. Stalin had hoped that this maneuver would force the western powers to retract the new currency. To the leading communist power, the western currency represented not only a provocative challenge to the formation of a socialist system in its zone of occupation, but also and above all, it signified the first step

The partition was introduced early: The sector boundary at Oberbaum Bridge (1948)

towards the establishment of an independent West German state. The Western Allies decided to provide their isolated sectors with food and provisions through an airlift. With the airlift, the war victors ceased to be regarded as occupying powers and were welcomed as the protectors of West Berlin.

Berlin's city government split in two after 1948 – two parliaments and two government administrations. The political division of the city was thus sealed. West Berlin, in the middle of the Soviet zone of occupation – and later the GDR– became the bone of contention between the world powers, and a permanent nuisance to the communist camp.

Despite the different currencies and economic systems, Berliners were still able to move freely throughout the entire city. The West naturally harbored the hope that its presence in the center of the GDR would infect its surroundings. And with this in mind, it generously nourished West Berlin back to health and made it the "showcase to the West." The East similarly favored East Berlin,

Uprising of the people in East Berlin on June 17, 1953

the capital of the GDR, over the other regions of the "real socialist" state. An ideological competition flared up, spurred on by propaganda. It was a race that the young GDR risked losing.

The state beyond the Elbe river was suffering from the loss of its population. More than 2.4 million people had turned their backs on communism between September 1949 and the day the Wall was built. They left because of the meager provisions and food in the East and because the "economic miracle" in West Germany was alluring. But they also fled the strong and prominent authority of the state, expropriation and political suppression, all of which made life in the GDR difficult. The easiest and safest way to the Federal Republic was over West Berlin. Just a short trip with public transportation and within minutes East Berliners were in another world system, in the enemy camp.

West Berlin, the outpost of the free world in the more or less one-party state of the GDR, was an island of prosperity in the middle of a problem-ridden planned economy, and it provided the best escape route from the GDR. West Berlin increasingly became a nuisance to the eastern bloc leaders. And so it came that a second Berlin crisis broke out in the end of the 1950s. On November 10,

1958, the Soviet head of state, Nikita Khrushchev, presented an ultimatum to the three western powers: "The western powers are to withdraw from Berlin within six months, until May 1959, and West Berlin is to be transformed into a demilitarized free city." This demand masked Khrushchev's desire to bring the western part of the city under the aegis of the GDR. Should the western powers refuse this solution, the Soviet Union would sign a separate peace accord with the GDR. This meant providing "sovereignty of land, water and air" to the GDR. The threat of another blockade of West Berlin was in the air. The western powers categorically rejected the ultimatum since the "free city" West Berlin, without the military support of the Allies would be defenseless and at the mercy of the Soviet and German communists.

The ultimatum expired without consequences. But it became more than ever clear that the Cold War in Berlin might erupt into a heated conflict at any moment. The situation in the GDR did not markedly improve and Berlin steered towards its greatest misfortune since the war. The SED (Socialist Unity Party) leadership wanted to put an end once and for all to the freedom of movement within the Berlin frontline city. The opening to West Berlin had to be finally closed. The

GDR began a vicious propaganda campaign against so-called "border-crossers," people who benefited from the different living standards in the two parts of the city (about 12,000 West Berliners worked in the eastern sector and 53,000 East Berliners worked in the western sector). In addition, the SED regime accused the West of engaging in "human trafficking," by deliberately wooing away qualified employees from the GDR.

The number of GDR refugees increased dramatically. In 1960 about 360,000 citizens left East Germany. In the first half of 1961, the number had already reached 160,000. The situation continued to escalate in the summer. In July, 30,400 people fled. In the first two weeks of August, approximately 47,400 people moved from the East to the West of Germany. If the GDR wanted to prevent the total economic and political collapse of its state, it would have to act soon.

That is why, on the night of August 13, 1961, in the Friedrichstrasse Station, the conductors shouted: "Everybody off. This train ends here!" It was the last stop for trains from the East before crossing to West. West Berlin was sealed off with barbed wire, soldiers and armored personnel carriers. An order was given to shoot anyone trying to escape from the GDR. During the Wall's 28 year history, well over a hundred people were killed trying to escape. More than 5,000 succeeded in making it to the other side. About 3,200 people were caught trying to escape. They were arrested and most of them received prison sentences of many years.

In its national propaganda, the SED leadership justified its building of the Wall as a defensive measure against "western imperialism." The border in their words was not a cage for its own population but an "Anti-Fascist Protective Wall" against the West. In early 1989, Erich Honecker, the GDR state and party leader and organizer of the construction of the Wall, proclaimed a long future for his work: The Wall will still stand in "50 and even in 100 years," he said.

But it turned out differently. The inhuman monstrosity was pulled down by the citizens of the GDR. On the night of November 9, 1989, Berlin celebrated the greatest victory of its recent history. Huge masses of people peacefully stormed the border-crossings. "Berlin's historical hour" ran the headlines of the extra editions. The socialist state collapsed and on October 3, 1990, Germany was unified.

The Brandenburg Gate as a symbol of the division (1966)

And the Wall at the Brandenburg Gate as a symbol of freedom on November 10, 1989

This unexpected event did not occur independent of the international political situation. The reform course in Moscow that Mikhael Gorbachev had introduced in 1985 set off a wave of citizens' protests throughout Eastern Europe. The GDR collapsed not from external pressure, but under internal strain. The year 1989 was a turning point in the history of Germany and Europe. Demands for democracy, freedom to travel, and diversity of opinion could no longer be repressed by the rulers of the GDR. The poor economic situation and meager supply of goods reinforced the discontentment of the population. Once again a wave of refugees left the country causing problems for the socialist state. And the SED government tottered. By the end of the year, almost all the intransigent communist regimes of the Warsaw Pact had been brought down by peaceful revolutions. The Iron Curtain that for years had divided Europe, Germany and Berlin, disappeared.

This book describes the different stages of the Berlin Wall from its construction, including the development of an extended border ground security system, to its role in Berlin daily life and finally, its collapse.

Speeches from politicians and historical documents convey the significance and explosive nature of Berlin. Special aspects such as Wall Art and the popular Wall souvenirs are also described.

Eight walking tours along the former "line of demarcation" provide the reader with an opportunity to gather an impressive look at the "passage of history" in Berlin.

The walks are an invitation to actively search for traces of the Wall and remains of the former border grounds. They lead the reader to the significant sites of the divided city, such as the Reichstag, Potsdamer Platz, Oberbaum Bridge, Checkpoint Charlie, East-Side-Gallery and Bernauer Strasse, and they also provide an overall impression of the sector boundaries.

Above all, however, this book gives people who personally experienced and were effected by the Wall in Berlin a chance to recount their memories of its construction, escape attempts, expulsion and the opening of the border.

For these people from the East and the West, the Wall is more than just a part of German history, it is a part of their own biography.

Building the Wall ... August 13, 1961

A mild summer night in Berlin. Nothing particularly unusual. All is quiet at headquarters of the West Berlin police. It is passed midnight. Even the first hour of August 13 remain uneventful. The city, situated between two power blocks, appears to be easing towards a peaceful Sunday.

Were it not for that strange incident on the S-Bahn commuter line. At 1:54 a.m. the Spandau police precinct reports to the situation center that the S-Bahn train coming from Staaken heading for Berlin was being turned back to "Soviet zone territory. Passengers had to leave the train and were given back their fare." A short time later the Wedding district reports that the S-Bahn train service at the Gesundbrunnen station has been disrupted.

The S-Bahn, an elevated transportation system that travels across all of Berlin, is administrated by the German Democratic Republic (GDR). That had been agreed upon by the four victorious allies after the war. So whatever happens with the S-Bahn is not the concern of the West Berlin authorities. And yet, in the city that had once been blockaded, authorities are sensitive to irregularities that occur at the sector boundaries.

And the situation worsens. All the reports coming in at twenty past two sound serious: "Fifteen military trucks with Vopos (People's Police) at the Oberbaum Bridge," "Armored scout cars at Sonnenallee," "Hundreds of Vopos and border guards armed with machine guns at Brandenburg Gate."

Troops are marching toward the border crossings in East Berlin! Are the communist troops about to march into West Berlin?

The island-city is at the moment practically without leadership. The Berlin mayor is campaigning through West Germany for the upcoming election. The situation center sounds the alarm. All of the 13,000 West Berlin police officers are pulled out of their beds. The people in charge try desperately to notify the mayor who just happens to be on an overnight train that at this very moment can not be reached.

Meanwhile the police watch bewildered as large numbers of uniformed men from East Berlin march to the line of demarcation between the east and west districts. And they are armed. And they are stringing barbed wire, tearing up the streets and erecting barriers.

The press has by now become informed of these extraordinary events: "Brandenburg Gate closed off," the Associated Press reports at 3:37 in the morning. At 3:53 the German press agency confirms: "Vopo putting up barbed wire." This Berlin summer night is becoming a nightmare. Only the residents are still oblivious to their own fate. They are sleeping.

At ten past one in the morning the East Berlin radio had interrupted its "Melodies at Night" program for a special announcement:

"The governments of the Warsaw Pact States approached the People's Chamber and the government of the GDR with the suggestion that measures be taken at the border to effectively remove the subversive activities directed against the countries of the socialist bloc and to secure reliable surveillance of the entire territory of West Berlin."

East Berlin is by now besieged by 8,000 soldiers of the GDR National People's Army. Erich Honecker is taking no risks. The 49-year-old SED party functionary and secretary of the National Defense Council wants to be absolutely sure that this surprise operation is pulled off without any interference from the population. Armored personnel carriers and combat tanks clatter along the main avenues of East Berlin. Their Destination: the sector boundary to the western territory.

The tanks halt one thousand meters from the sector boundary. The 10,500 People's Police and Border Guards are reinforced by the army as they continue their advance towards enemy territory, positioning themselves exactly along the invisible borderline.

In his command station at the police headquarters at Alexanderplatz, Honecker evaluates the reports coming in. Everything is running according to plan.

The necessary orders had been signed on August 12 by Walter Ulbricht, head of the SED and chairman of the GDR Council of State. At the Brandenburg Gate, the proud

Walter Ulbricht *(chairman of the GDR Council of State), press conference, June 15, 1961*

Doherr, a correspondent of the Frankfurter Rundschau, asks Ulbricht whether the aim of the GDR to achieve a free city in West Berlin means "erecting a state border at the Brandenburg Gate." He answers:

I understand your question to imply that there are people in West Germany who would like to see us mobilize the construction workers of the capital of the GDR for the purpose of building a wall. I am not aware of any such intention. The construction workers of our city are for the most part busy building apartment houses, and their working capacities are fully employed to that end. Nobody intends to put up a wall.

The Wall was built through Berlin piece by piece. Construction on Lindenstrasse on August 18, 1961

The GDR leadership had Berlin in its sights on Bernauer Strasse on August 14, 1961

landmark of a once confident city, eerie scenes are unfolding. Military cars illuminate the darkness. In the dim headlights, armed men transform the plaza into a battlefield. Lining up rows of combat tanks. Erecting barriers of barbed wire and concrete stakes.

The nightmare will continue for another 28 years. But the citizens of Berlin don't know this yet. They are sleeping.

The sun is about to rise when the mayor of Berlin, Willy Brandt, travelling in an overnight train, is awoken. It is 4:30 a.m. He takes the first flight out of Nuremberg and returns to his besieged city. Enraged and fearful. The SPD politician, who was 48 years old at the time, later recalls: "We drove to Potsdamer Platz and to Brandenburg Gate, we saw the same picture everywhere: construction workers, barriers, concrete posts, barbed wire, GDR military." The barriers are lined up along a 160 kilometer long strip dividing West

Berlin from East Berlin and the surrounding GDR. Of the 81 streets that had connected the east and west sectors, only 12 are still open. The elevated and underground public transportation systems have been cut off between the two city sections.

A slap in the face for the three western powers, France, Great Britain and the USA: The protectors and leaders of the west sectors of Berlin are apparently caught off guard. Berlin, the old bone of contention between the two super powers, the permanent trouble spot in the cold war between the East and West, – will it set off a war between the Soviet Union and the United States?

The president of the United States, John F. Kennedy, is informed of the situation at 12:30 p.m. local time while aboard his yacht on the Atlantic coast. He responds calmly. He gives a statement to the press: "The blockade of East Berlin is a visible sign of the defeat of the communist system for all the world to

see. Ulbricht's East German regime bears responsibility to the world for the inhumane imprisonment of its own population." There was no other reaction, no demands, no ultimatum. He later explains the restrained response of the western world to his close circle of advisors: "The other side panicked – but not we. We are going to do nothing now because the only alternative is war. It's all over. They are not going to overrun Berlin."

Even Chancellor Adenauer responds with unusual defensiveness: Although he protests strongly, he doesn't interrupt his election campaign. He waits a week before coming to the cordoned off city.

The shocked Berlin population – both in East and West – is unwilling to accept the extreme situation that has been thrust upon them. In *Neues Deutschland*, the East German party paper, the SED leadership commends the apparent good conduct of the sealed in population. "Since Sunday border posts are

Confrontation at Checkpoint Charlie. US tanks on October 26, 1961

in place at the border. The GDR population protects these posts because these posts provide the GDR population with the best protection against the West German militarists." But on the streets, in the factories and along the new marked border, the GDR population is in truth more rebellious than the insolent communist propaganda is willing to admit. There are isolated protests, even clashes with the People's Police. In the factory halls, machinery suddenly comes to a halt. Resistance disguised as repair work. The surveillance apparatus of the SED regime has its hands full trying to silence the critical and courageous voices. In just the last two weeks in August, thousands of people are arrested for voicing protest against the border divide.

In the democratic western part of the city, Berliners vent their anger freely: "With unprecedented frivolity, Khrushchev and Ulbricht have over the weekend transformed the Soviet zone and the east sector of Berlin

Willy Brandt *(mayor of Berlin), August 16, 1961 in front of the Schöneberg city hall*

The Soviet Union loosened the reins a bit on its watchdog Ulbricht. It allowed him to march his troops into the eastern sector of this city (…)

An unlawful regime has committed another injustice, one worse than any before. The East bears responsibility! It bears the full responsibility for what may follow as a result. But we can't allow ourselves to be content with this mere observation. A shouting protest cannot lead solely to a written protest. The protest of the three western commandants was good, but it must not be left just at that. (…)

I consciously turn in this hour to the people of this country who work in the administrations and organizations of the zone regime, and I turn in particular to those serving in the military units of the zone regime. (…)

Don't allow yourselves to be reduced to rabble! Behave humanely whenever possible, and above all, do not shoot at your own countrymen.

We are not able to lift this burden that weighs upon the shoulders of our fellow-citizens in the sector and our countrymen in the zone these days, and that is the hardest part for us! We can only help them to bear it by showing that we are big enough for this hour! They ask if we are writing them off now. There is only one answer: No, never! They ask if we will betray them now. And to this there is also only one answer: No, never!

Our people are being put to a test, a real test that makes everything that has happened in the last years seem trivial! Our people will now be judged by history, and heaven forbid, if out of indifference, convenience, sluggishness or moral weakness, we don't rise to the occasion! Because then the Communists won't stop at the Brandenburg Gate. They will also not stop at the zone border and not at the Rhine! (…)

We are not afraid. Today I wrote a personal letter to the president of the United States, John Kennedy, and openly expressed my, and I believe our view, that Berlin expects more than words. Berlin expects political action. We appeal to all peoples of the world, we call on all their representatives, to come here to Berlin to see them try to cover a bleeding wound with barbed wire and army boots. Here they can witness the reality and severe brutality of a system that promised the people paradise on earth and then smothers the flight of these people from this paradise by a mass contingent of troops. The world is only as moral as the morality found in Berlin.

The right to self-determination is nowhere in the world secure as long as the right to self-determination of our people is denied. We will never tire of demanding and fighting for this right for ourselves until we have attained it. This struggle has now become much more difficult. (…)

Europe and the entire world is watching us. We must conduct ourselves in a way that the enemy is not pleased and our countrymen do not despair. More than ever before we must stick together and stay together. We must prove that we are worthy of the ideals that the freedom bell over our heads symbolizes. We must stand up, calmly, but with determination and a strong will, for all of Germany, for unity and justice and freedom.

An end to the freedom of movement. In August 1961, border guards controlled Friedrichstrasse

into a huge concentration camp, forcing six million people behind the barbed wire of the communist dictatorship," Karl Silex, editor-in-chief of *Der Tagesspiegel* newspaper writes. On August 16, the *Bild-Zeitung* condemns the inaction of the Western Allies and runs the headline "The West does NOTHING!" That is the day that 300,000 Berliners demonstrate against the closing of the border in front of the Schöneberg city hall, where the West Berlin government resides. They show the leaders in the East that they won't be intimidated and angrily let the leaders in the West know that they feel deserted by their "protectors." The mood is tense when Willy Brandt gives his speech before the West Berlin population. Posters proclaim "Deceived by the West."

Now Washington responds. On August 19, Kennedy sends his deputy, the vice-president Lyndon B. Johnson, to Berlin. At the same time, as a pointed gesture, 1500 American soldiers are sent to reinforce the Berlin US-garrison, and travel over the transit route across the GDR to West Berlin. The soldiers and Johnson are given a tumultuous welcome. The American vice-president is accompanied by General Lucius D. Clay, who is fondly remembered in Berlin as the organizer of the airlift of 1948–49. Kennedy takes the Berlin crisis seriously and demonstrates strength. In October, Clay will be confronted and master the first and only direct confrontation between the world powers (see tour: Checkpoint Charlie).

Meanwhile the GDR proceeds to erect a barrier around West Berlin and Walter Ulbricht, chairman of the GDR Council of State, declares it to be a "measure towards securing peace."

On August 23, the border crossings are reduced to seven: Bornholmer Strasse, Chausseestrasse, Invalidenstrasse, Heinrich-Heine-Strasse, Oberbaum Bridge, Sonnenallee and Checkpoint Charlie. Heavily guarded crossings reserved only for diplomats, representatives of the Allies or citizens of West Germany. The West Berlin residents are prohibited by the GDR government from entering East Berlin. Berliners, friends and families are separated for years. The city is paralyzed in a state of shock.

Contemporary Witness . . . Miriam Flotow

While listening to the news on the radio on Sunday afternoon, I was completely startled. I even became nauseous. East Berlin sealed off! Just four days earlier I had lived there. Together with my ex-husband in Köpenick. I had separated from him in the week before the Wall was built. I had moved with him there, but soon returned to Charlottenburg, my home district. Had I delayed my decision to leave him just a few more days – who knows what would have become of me.

In the summer of 1961 nobody was expecting the SED government to get serious. No one could have imagined that what Walter Ulbricht had indirectly announced would actually happen. The sentence: "Nobody intends to put up a wall." In West Berlin we simply didn't take it seriously.

That evening I drove with friends to Bernauer Strasse. The atmosphere was oppressive. There were many people there, standing dumbfounded, looking at the barrier of barbed wire and soldiers. Many people were crying, waving to relatives. I, too, had an aunt in the East. It never crossed my mind that I wouldn't see her again for years.

We were all very emotional on this evening. But we were still certain that the whole commotion would be over soon. Even now with the city divided in two. No one thought that the division would last almost three decades. On August 13 no one was able to foresee how painful the reality would be.

Until gradually everything became more radically sealed off. And suddenly they had built a real wall. Piece for piece. When the Wall and watchtowers were built, it became even more oppressive in the city.

Sometimes we had the impression that the victorious powers had agreed on the action beforehand. I was scared. Scared of another war. I had a packed suitcase under my bed filled with everything I might need. Just in case. In case my family and I had to flee. The memory of the war was still

very vivid to me. That is why nobody seriously wanted the Western Allies to march off and tear down the barricade.

The Wall had decisive consequences for my family and me. At the time of its construction I was working for a tailor. Although the economic wonder had by now reached West Berlin, my wages were very low. I was paid 40 marks per week. My father worked for the Reichsbahn (railway) that had belonged to the GDR, so he received half of his salary in East currency. Shopping in the East was a less expensive alternative for us. Before the Wall was built I used to exchange my German marks for East marks so that I could buy bread, meat and sausage in the East. Of course the selection was meager there. But I never considered that I was taking something away from the easterners.

It was commonplace in Berlin to take advantage of the economic inequality. There were also bordercrossers from the East who worked for low wages in the West and continued to live for low rent in the East. They were better off with their West money than other residents in the East. But many westerners resented that they worked for less money than

the westerners. They said "the bordercrossers are taking our jobs away."

Shopping trips to the West were not without risk. They were illegal. I had to watch out for the random checks by the People's Police.

Even clothing, fabric and shoes were cheaper in the East. The selection was considerably worse, but less expensive. That is why I often purchased fabric for sewing. Although I often went to the East I had little to do with the people there. The two societies had by then grown completely apart. There were extreme differences due to the poor economic situation in the East. The West was enticing, and the refugee camps in West Berlin were filled to the brim in 1961.

All that was over on August 13. My family now had to manage with a little less. In the factories and businesses in the West, the colleagues from the East were suddenly gone. Bad news came every day. The newspapers were filled with reports of escapes. A friend of mine worked in a factory close to the Wall in Reinickendorf. A part of the Borsig factory was located there in the East and the wall around the property grounds suddenly became the border. Everyday my friend saw workers climbing over the barbed wire fence. For a long time there was even a hidden door in the factory wall. Former colleagues from the East came through it undetected. All the sudden they showed up at work and said "I'm staying in the West!"

Although my family and I were worse off, and although the future was uncertain, I never thought about leaving Berlin. We would not have left because of the threatening situation. Most of the West Germans were more scared of the East regime than we in Berlin who were directly affected by it. The SED government had to close the gap to West Berlin, otherwise the GDR would have bled to death. Even years later, I never had the feeling of being locked in.

Wall against the People … Extension of the Wall … Wall Victims

Conrad Schumann ten years after his flight standing in front of the famous photo of his leap over barbed wire at Bernauer Strasse (left) and just shortly before his escape on August 15, 1961

Standing on Ruppiner Strasse, the 19-year-old Conrad Schumann is forced to listen to the people swearing at him, calling him "traitor" and "concentration camp guard." He wrestles with himself, wondering whether it is right that he is standing there, fulfilling his duty. With helmet, carbine and the uniform of the National People's Army. Marching up and down along the low barbed wire barrier with a gun, preventing the people on Bernauer Strasse from entering the Wedding district.

The barrier was erected just 48 hours ago on the orders of his supervisors. At some point Schumann is standing a good distance from the other soldiers on guard duty. He decides to take off, jumping with one leap over the barbed wire and throwing his weapon off his shoulder. He keeps running until he reaches a West Berlin police van. He is out of danger.

The photo of the young soldier leaping over the border goes around the world and makes clear what the "Anti-Fascist Protective Wall" really is and who the obstacles and barriers are really directed against. Against the

citizens of the GDR. Schumann is the first Wall refugee to become famous. In the first six weeks after the border is closed another 85 border guards flee to the West.

By August 13, as many as 1.6 million GDR citizens had left the socialist state through West Berlin. After that anyone who wanted to turn their back on the "real socialism" had to undertake a dangerous escape. Jumping over barbed wire, crawling through fences, swimming across canals or the Spree river. Or even jumping out apartment house windows.

An estimated one thousand people flee in panic and unexpectedly during the first four weeks after August 13. They leave their friends, families and possessions behind them.

A perverse race begins between the SED regime and the GDR citizens and keeps Berlin in suspense. On August 15, the day that Conrad Schumann succeeds in jumping over the barbed wire in a single leap, the border troops began removing the temporary barrier and replacing it with a wall crowned with barbed wire and as high as a man. The

Wall grows meter by meter. The barrier, sealing off the country, has to be impermeable. Invincible.

People lose their lives in the first days of the struggle against the Wall. For instance at Bernauer Strasse. The buildings along the southern side of the street belong to the eastern sector, but the sidewalk in front is in the West. The building fronts are the border. Many people jump from their windows or slide down a rope because their apartment windows are being walled up.

On August 19, Rudolf Urban attempts to slide down from his apartment window and falls to the ground. He dies a short time later from his injuries.

On August 22, the 59-year-old Ida Siekmann jumps from the third floor and misses the mattress that has been laid out to catch her fall. She suffers fatal injuries. These are the first victims of the Wall.

The dramatic scenes at Bernauer Strasse don't stop. On September 24, 1961, the People's Police and Stasi (State Security Service) attempt to pull a 77-year-old women who has climbed out of her window back into the building. The West Berlin fire department arrives to provide a safety net for the refugees to jump into.

Residential areas became military prohibited zones; apartment buildings became guard buildings (1963)

Dramatic escapes took place at Bernauer Strasse (August 1961)

An act of desperation comes to an end: Thousands were arrested while attempting to escape and were sent to prison (August 1962)

A powerful truck successfully broke through the Wall at Boyenstrasse in Wedding in April 1962

The GDR finally resolves to proceed harshly against the border houses that are being used for escapes. At the end of September, all 2,000 residents who are still residing in the building are forced to evacuate. Building entrances and windows are permanently walled off.

On August 24 it becomes brutally clear that the SED is no longer willing to accept the continued escapes across the border. Nine days earlier Conrad Schumann took his leap to freedom and then told the West Berlin police what orders were given to the soldiers of the People's Army.

"There were only three instructions: We were not allowed to let anyone in our border area leave the eastern sector for the West; we were not to respond to provocations from the West; and we were not allowed to fire real bullets."

But on August 24 for the first time soldiers shoot real bullets.

In the afternoon. Another summer day. Not far from the Friedrichstrasse train station, a young man is running towards the Humboldt Harbor. The basin is situated within the border territory. A guard shoots two warning shots, but the man continues to run and jumps into the harbor basin. More shots. And this time the guard aimed. The 24-year-old tailor, Günter Litfin, floats motionless in the water. He is dead. Günter Litfin is the first refugee to be killed by a GDR border guard.

What he couldn't know: Just two days before, the SED politburo gave the order "that any violation of the border to our German Democratic Republic, even – out of necessity – will be answered with the call of firearms."

On August 29, Roland Hoff is shot to death while attempting to swim across the Teltow Canal.

Final escape route: When security at the border increased, many people tried to flee to freedom through underground tunnels (1962)

By the end of October 1961, fifteen people have lost their lives at the border to West Berlin. Despite international protests against the shooting at the Wall, the GDR regime does not retract its order to shoot.

Three quarters of a year before the fall of the Wall, on the night of February 5, 1989, border soldiers shoot and kill the 20-year-old young man, Chris Gueffroy, in Berlin-Treptow as he attempts to flee.

He is the last refugee to be shot. On May 8, 1989, Winfried Freudenberg attempts to escape in his self-made hot air balloon. He crashes over Zehlendorf and dies.

Between 100 and 150 people lose their lives at the Wall during the 28 years of its existence.

Because these incidents were kept secret by the GDR, it has not yet been possible to establish a more exact count.

Fleeing from the GDR was a very dangerous undertaking.

Escapes from the GDR required increasingly refined, creative and secret planning. In the first years after August 13, 1961, tunnels were dug between the East and the West, automobiles were equipped with hiding places, false foreign passports were acquired.

Over years the GDR systematically built up the border facilities with watchtowers and patrol paths (Spandau 1981)

The operations were often prepared by "escape helpers" living in West Berlin. At first they acted out of a love for freedom or for political reasons, and later also for money.

Many operations failed or were betrayed by spies of the GDR State Security Service. Countless escape-helpers were arrested and sentenced to long prison terms for "illegal human trafficking." More than 3,200 people were arrested while attempting to flee and generally received long prison terms.

New generation of the Wall. The pipe construction made it more difficult to climb over (Wedding 1981)

Spectacular escape attempts angered the GDR regime.

For example in 1964, when nine people successively escaped in a BMW-Isetta. After that cars at the border were painstakingly examined, even under the hood.

In 1961 a passenger train succeeded in breaking through the Wall. On December 5, on route from Hamburg to Berlin, a steam engine carrying thirty-two passengers rammed through the barrier. Everyone made it to West Berlin territory uninjured.

In 1966 two East Berliners tore down a piece of the Wall with a bulldozer – then it was still possible to push down the Wall. Well into the 1980s incidents of vehicles breaking through the Wall were still making the headlines. For example on March 10, 1988, when at two in the morning, a large truck from Potsdam crashed into the Glienicker Bridge and broke through a number of concrete barriers. Three men from Babelsberg made it safely to West Berlin.

Even a ship was used to escape. On the morning of June 7, 1962, the "Friedrich Wolf" departed from the Treptow mooring. A group of refugees sort of kidnapped the passenger steamer. Upon approaching the Oberbaum Bridge, the ship suddenly took a sharp turn into the Landwehr Canal towards West Berlin. Although the ship was shot at, the "pirates" made it safely to the savior island-city.

By 1989, the number of successful escape attempts had reached approximately 5000, 574 of them were undertaken by members of the armed units.

Impermeable, invincible.

Over time the leaders of the GDR built their national border into a perfected, frightening fortress. It began with barbed wire and soon steel tank barricades and a wall of cavity blocks followed.

By November 1961, meter wide concrete plates were piled on top of one another, for example in front of the Brandenburg Gate, where the border was unexpectedly slightly lower than elsewhere.

Watchtowers were erected. Buildings that stood in the border area were torn down. Graveyards were flattened and built over. The underground canalization system was barricaded. The GDR leadership had military lanes

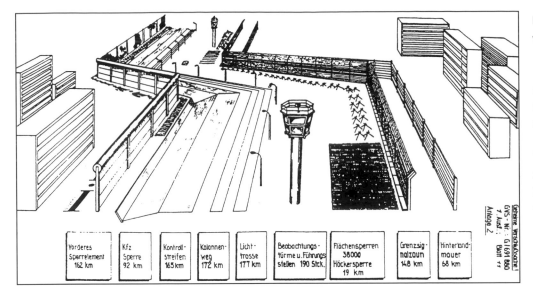

Diagram of perfected border grounds. In the end the "Wall" was a many-layered system of obstacles

| Vorderes Sperrelement 162 km | Kfz Sperre 92 km | Kontroll-streifen 165 km | Kolonnen-weg 172 km | Licht-trasse 177 km | Beobachtungs-türme u.Führungs stellen 190 Stck. | Flächensperren 38000 Höckersperre 19 km | Grenzsig-nalzaun 148 km | Hinterland-mauer 68 km |

carved through the city. With each month the gigantic structure became more monstrous, more effective and more dangerous.

The "Wall" ultimately consisted of many different elements. There was the wall on the border to West Berlin and the "hinterland wall" on the east side. Between them stood:

- an illuminated control strip, the death strip, usually between 6 and 15 meters wide
- anti-vehicle ditches or Spanish riders

John F. Kennedy *(United States president), June 26, 1963, in front of the Schöneberg city hall*

Dear Berliners!
Two thousand years ago the proudest boast was "Civitas Romanus sum." Today, in the world of freedom, the proudest boast is "Ich bin ein Berliner." (…)

There are many people in the world who really don't understand, or say they don't, what is the great issue between the free world and the Communist world. Let them come to Berlin..

There are some who say that Communism is the way of the future. Let them come to Berlin.

And there are some who say in Europe and elsewhere we can work with the Communists. Let them come to Berlin.

And there are even a few who say that it is true that Communism is an evil system, but it permits us to make economic progress. "Lasst sie nach Berlin kommen."

Freedom has many difficulties and democracy is not perfect, but we have never had to put a wall up to keep our people in, to prevent them from leaving us.

I want to say, on behalf of my countrymen, who live many miles away on the other side of the Atlantic, who are far distant from you, that they take the greatest pride that they have been able to share with you, even from a distance, the story of the last eighteen years. I know of no town, no city, that has been besieged for eighteen years that still lives with the vitality and the force, and the hope and the determination of the city of West Berlin. While the Wall is the most obvious and vivid demonstration of the failures of the Communist system, for all the world to see, we take no satisfaction in it, for it is an offence not only against history but an offence against humanity, separating families, dividing husbands and wives and brothers and sisters, and dividing a people who wish to be joined together. What is true of this city is true of Germany – real, lasting peace in Europe can

never be assured as long as one German out of four is denied the elementary right of free men, and that is to make a free choice. (…)

You live in a defended island of freedom, but your life is part of the main. So let me ask you, as I close, to lift your eyes beyond the dangers of today to the hopes of tomorrow, beyond the freedom merely of this city of Berlin, or your country of Germany, to the advance of freedom everywhere, beyond the Wall to the day of peace with justice, (…).

Freedom is indivisible, and when one man is enslaved, all are not free. When all are free, then we can look forward to that day when this city will be joined as one – and this country, and this great continent of Europe – in a peaceful and hopeful glow. When that day finally comes, as it will, the people of West Berlin can take sober satisfaction in the fact that they were in the front lines for almost two decades.

All free men, wherever they may live, are citizens of Berlin, and, therefore, as a free man, I take pride in the words: "Ich bin ein Berliner."

- five meter high light masts
- a control path for the patrol cars
- a sensor and signal fence which set off an alarm when touched
- watchtowers, bunkers, tripwire, shooting sites and dog runs.

The death strip was patrolled in regular intervals by two border soldiers as part of the surveillance.

Final measures to extend and reinforce the Wall began in 1976. The square blocks and concrete girders on the west side were replaced by a 3.6 meter high wall made of prefabricated concrete plates.

This wall, referred to as the "4th generation" or in official jargon as "Wall 75" would characterize the division until 1989. The individual concrete segments were generally 3.6 meters high, 1.20 meters wide and 15 centimeters thick.

An asbestos concrete pipe (40 centimeters in diameter) rested on the top of the wall, making it difficult to mount with a ladder or other instrument.

A 2.10 meter projecting "foot" shaped like an abutment secured a high level of stability. Not even a massive truck could breach through it now.

An estimated 45,000 concrete segments, at a price of 359 GDR marks per piece, were erected around West Berlin.

A tall tightly meshed metal lattice fence often stood in place of the concrete wall in rural areas along the outer border of West Berlin.

Metal boards with sharp upward pointing nails were placed beneath the barrier inside the control strip at some sites.

In the summer of 1989, the 155 kilometer long border ring around West Berlin consisted of:

- concrete plates (106 kilometers)
- metal fence 83 (66.5 kilometer)
- anti-vehicle ditches (105 kilometers)
- sensor fence (127 kilometer)
- patrol path (124 kilometer)
- 302 watchtowers
- 20 bunkers
- 259 dog runs

By August 21, 1961 the first concrete slabs had already been put to use in the construction of the Wall on Bernauer Strasse (corner of Ackerstraße)

could get his mother and sister out of East Berlin as well. He arranged fake passports for them that identified them as Austrian citizens and in November 1961 they were able to leave sealed off East Berlin without being detected.

Through the organization that provided the passports Rudolph and his friend met two Italians who had friends in East Berlin. A couple with a child. They said they wanted to get their friends out of the GDR.

"Having myself been a refugee, I knew how immense the mental trauma of living in the isolated GDR was. That's why I wanted to help." The two Italians had the idea of building a tunnel to East Berlin. There had been plenty of escape tunnels by then. But they had all been quite simple or short. But with security at the border increasing with each passing week, only a major underground construction had a chance of success. The Italians envisioned a 180 meter long escape tunnel that would cross beneath Bernauer Strasse, where the southern buildings made up the border boundary, and continue beneath the buildings and the next street to the end of the adjacent housing block on Rheinsberger Strasse.

"You are nuts," a friend of ours who studied engineering commented after hearing about the daring plan.

"We wouldn't be talked out of our idea," Rudolph recalls. Work was to begin after the winter. Old factory grounds at the corner of Bernauer Strasse and Brunnenstrasse were to serve as the starting point for the underground construction. When the group asked the owner if they could rent a spacious cellar, he suspected what they were up to. "Man," he said cheerfully, "why didn't you come sooner?! It is about time somebody showed them over there a thing or two." Thrilled with their intentions, he let them use the cellar for free.

It was a huge cellar, perfect for the job. "We used maps from the land registry office to find the best route to East Berlin." They began work in the spring of 1962. Five of them chiseled out the concrete base of the cell. Using spades and pickaxes, they worked their way into the soil. They first dug three meters deep into the clay.

They only worked at night for fear that the border guards on the other side of Bernauer Strasse might become suspicious. After all, they observed every coming and going on the west side. But soon the tunnel construction became a full-time job. Underground progress was slow. That is why they ended up digging around the clock. Three eight hour work shifts, seven days a week. The group had meanwhile grown to three or four people per shift. More and more helpers joined. And their fear of the Argus eyes of the GDR border guards grew since the more people who entered the factory grounds, the greater the danger of being discovered. So they reduced the operation to two shifts of twelve hours each. Between one and three meters were dug out each day.

Since the Italians were allowed to travel to the eastern part without being checked, they were able to keep their East Berlin friends informed of every detail of the progress.

Rudolf recalls: "The work in the 90 centimeter narrow one meter deep vault was a tremendous psychic strain." But everything ran perfectly: the air circulation functioned, the supports stayed in place. Until one day water seeped into the tunnel. The work had to stop.

It took weeks and a great amount of energy to pump the water out of the underground passage. But it wasn't only nature that caused problems. Word of the operation had spread. Forty people now contributed to the project. At any point a GDR spy might show up on the grounds. Something had to be done. Time was running out.

A small group changed the plan. "The route of the tunnel was shortened." The escape route would now end just one block behind the border on Schönholzer Strasse. This was a risky decision because the Schönholzer Strasse was in the heavily guarded border area. A barbed wire fence along the middle of the street divided the street in two. Only residents were allowed to enter the buildings whose back sections bordered on Bernauer Strasse, the highly sensitive security area of the Berlin Wall.

In order to reach the unguarded section, the tunnel had to at least cross under Schönholzer Strasse. In the end it was about 120 meters long. "We knew approximately where we would come up," recalls Rudolph. But they could only establish exactly which building cellar they had entered after the first cut. The twenty-nine refugees who were planning to escape on the first day had to know the exact street address.

When they were certain that they had reached the unguarded section of Schönholzer Strasse, they dug about two and half meters diagonally upward. On September 14, 1962, Rudolf explains, it happened. A dim light pierced into the escape tunnel from the cellar. "We were through!"

Now they had to move very fast. The people who were planning to flee were ready. But they still didn't know which building would lead them into the West. Three of the tunnel builders cautiously approached the cellar door and picked it open. The coast was clear. "I had to go to the front entrance and see which house it was. And to do this I had to go out on to Schönholzer Strasse." Without a clue of what was awaiting him on the other side of the heavy door.

Rudolph saw the border guards patrolling the street. He read: Schönholzer Strasse 7.

The refugees, close relatives and friends from all over the GDR were informed. In small groups they assembled one after the other in the heavily guarded area. The first arrived at about 6 p.m. and then every fifteen minutes another small group followed. The last one sneaked through the door at around ten thirty at night. Nerves were on edge.

They were extremely lucky. "Not for one second we were in a serious or dangerous situation," Rudolph explains. The refugees did everything that they were told to do. No one hesitated to crawl into the narrow entrance. "In moments like that you just turn off your brain and your fears." Arriving on the other side in the West, they were greeted by the cameras of NBC, the American television network, which had purchased the film rights to the tunnel story. The amazed cameramen filmed young people and pensioners crawling exhausted but ecstatic out of the tunnel. There was even a four month old baby among them.

But while the first refugees were joyfully embraced, a catastrophe occurred underground. There was another water break. The last refugees had to crawl on their knees in a hurry through the mud. Although the water seeped into the tunnel relatively quickly, all 29 people made it. But the water put an end to the tunnel as an escape route. "There was nothing more we could do," Rudolph said.

What they didn't know was that the tunnel was not immediately discovered by the border troop lookouts. Fourteen days would pass before the walkway on Schönholzer Strasse caved in drawing attention to it. It had been beyond the imagination of the GDR State Security Service that such a thing was possible: a tunnel that was dug from the West and reached all the way into eastern territory.

Joachim Rudolph lives with his wife in West Berlin. The spectacular tunnel escape was filmed and broadcast on television.

Rapprochement ... Visitor Permits ... Four-Power Status ... Daily Life

A Sunday afternoon outing in the shadow of terror (Kreuzberg 1981)

What was life with the Wall like in a divided and partially enclosed city? It is hard to give an exact answer since there were always two views of the border in divided Berlin. West Berliners suddenly lived in a hermetically sealed "island," but they could leave it at any time and enter Western Europe. They could travel and – albeit with restrictions – even visit the eastern section of the city and the GDR. East Berliners, on the other hand, were "only" denied access to the western part of the city, but they were forced to live in a state that for the most part they rejected. The GDR was a dictatorship and prohibited its citizens from traveling to the democratic parts of Europe, above all to the Federal Republic of Germany. The division also radically reinforced the different living standards in the two societies. What both populations shared, however, was an ability to acclimate them-

selves to the new situation in the German capital, an extreme situation that would last for 28 years. The Berliners in the East and in the West had to come to terms with the unnatural division – whether they liked it or not.

For West Berlin, after the shock of August 13, 1961 subsided, coming to terms on the political level meant making the Wall as permeable as possible. Berliners on both sides, however, were not permitted to enter the other half. With its "policy of small steps," the West Berlin Senate tried to find a way to bring people, families and friends on both sides of the city together again and to put an end to the crisis-prone confrontational situation between the two systems in Berlin. A

For a long time separated families and friends had only visual contact. Bernauer Strasse 1962

long and tiresome negotiating process began that progressed slowly on delicate and shaky diplomatic ground since Berlin continued to play a central role in international political conflicts between the two superpowers. It took ten years before an agreement could be reached: In the Four-Power Accord of 1972 all sides agreed to accept and respect the status quo in Berlin.

The first major and on human terms important breakthrough in relations between the two halves of the city occurred much earlier, at Christmas 1963. More than two years after the Wall was built, West Berliners were finally permitted to again enter the eastern section of the city. But only according to a rigid arrangement that had been worked out during complicated negotiations between the West Berlin Senate and the GDR government.

The special visiting regulations were valid for a period of less than three weeks, from December 18, 1963 to January 5, 1964. Each entry permit was valid for a single day, from 6 in the morning until midnight. And every visitor, upon entering the East, had to exchange ten West German marks into GDR marks at a rate of 1:1. The largest obstacle, however, proved to be the distribution of "visitor permits" by the GDR authorities on West Berlin territory. The GDR postal workers accepted the applications in West Berlin. They were then processed in East Berlin and distributed at West Berlin schools and sports halls. Despite the icy cold and snow, long lines formed at the distribution locations where people waited for hours.

An article in the West Berlin daily paper, *Der Tagesspiegel*, described the situation: "At 1 p.m. about 32,000 Berliners waited in line at the sports halls, many of them had been standing for more than 12 hours in temperatures of 4 degrees or lower. The mood according to all reports was more agitated than on previous days. At 3 p.m. about 9,000 people who were waiting gave up hope of ever receiving their permit."

To get the onslaught under control, the GDR authorities increased the number of postal workers at the distribution sites. In the end a total of 1.2 million visitor permits for a day visit were issued during this two week period.

The experience of being reunited after two years of forced separation remains deeply ingrained in the memory of the city. There were tearful scenes on the temporary border crossings at Oberbaum Bridge and the Friedrichstrasse station. West Berliners, bearing dozens of presents and care packages, were overwhelmed by emotion as they greeted their relatives in East Berlin.

But this Christmastime family cheer remained an exception. Only four visitor permit agreements were made by summer 1966. Negotiations failed when the GDR attempted to link humane improvement with political demands that both West Berlin and the Western Allies, for reasons of legal status, were unable to accept. Access to East Berlin was closed off again after the summer of 1966 and not until a political "phase of reconciliation" began between the NATO states and the Warsaw Pact was a new agreement reached that made life in the divided city both more bearable and more reliable.

In March 1970, the cold war adversaries held a meeting in the former control council building in Berlin-Schöneberg (Kleistpark, today's constitutional court). The United States, Great Britain, France and the Soviet Union wanted to put aside once and for all the persistent quarrels over questions of status, checks at access routes to West Berlin and visitor regulations. The victorious powers of World War II conducted hard negotiations for over a year and a half until they reached an agreement in September 1971. With the Four-Power Accord that came into effect in 1972, Berlin ceased to be a bone of

Ronald Reagan *(United States president), June 12, 1987, at the 750th anniversary celebration, in front of the Brandenburg Gate*

(…) President von Weizsäcker has said, "The German question is open as long as the Brandenburg Gate is closed." Today I say: As long as the gate is closed, as long as this scar of a wall is permitted to stand, it is not the German question alone that remains open, but the question of freedom for all mankind. Yet I do not

come here to lament. For I find in Berlin a message of hope, even in the shadow of this wall, a message of triumph. (…)

In the 1950s, Khrushchev predicted: "We will bury you." But in the West today, we see a free world that has achieved a level of prosperity and well-being unprecedented in all human history. (…)

And now the Soviets themselves may, in a limited way, becoming to understand the importance of freedom. We hear much from Moscow about a new policy of reform and openness. Are these the beginnings of profound changes in the Soviet state? Or are they token gestures, intended to raise false hopes in the West, or to strengthen the Soviet system without changing it? (…)

General Secretary Gorbachev, if you seek peace, if you seek prosperity for the Soviet Union and Eastern Europe, if you seek liberalization: Come here to this gate! Mr. Gorbachev, open this gate! Mr. Gorbachev, tear down this wall! (…)

As I looked out a moment ago from the Reichstag, that embodiment of German unity, I noticed words crudely spray-painted upon the wall, perhaps a young Berliner: "This wall will fall. Beliefs become reality." Yes, across Europe, this wall will fall. For it cannot withstand faith; it cannot withstand truth. The wall cannot withstand freedom.

contention between the world powers. It no longer caused critical confrontations as it had 1948, 1958 and 1961 and the latent danger of war breaking out over Berlin subsided once and for all.

For West Berlin this was a diplomatic breakthrough that provided considerable relief from the pressures of daily life. On the basis of this agreement, the West Berlin Senate and the GDR were also able to negotiate a permanent arrangement for visits to East Berlin: West Berliners were now permitted to travel to the eastern section of the city thirty days a year. They had to apply in advance at a specific border-crossing and leave the East by midnight. The socialist leadership capitalized on the large number of West Berlin visitors to the GDR capital by requiring each visitor upon entering to exchange a predetermined amount of West German marks for GDR marks. The amount of this "minimum exchange" continued to increase over the years. In 1980, when the fee had reached 25 DM per person, the number of visits cut down from more than 3 million to 1.5 million.

After the Four-Power Accord came into effect, the situation in the divided city normalized and became more routine but it never ceased to be an extreme situation accompanied by many restrictions. The West Berliners became accustomed to their strange situation. After a time, they stopped feeling the presence of the Wall – it had become part of their lives. Friendships and romances also continued to exist across the border despite the Wall.

There were also a number of peculiarities along the Wall, such as the exclaves. Exclaves were areas that belonged to West Berlin but were situated outside the city on GDR territory. Steinstücken, for example, was a 13 hectare exclave with 130 residents in southeast Berlin. After the Wall was built, Steinstücken was abruptly cut off from the "mainland." The only connection to West Berlin was a 1.1 kilometer long path that was now blocked by barbed wire. For a month after the Wall was built, helicopters of the American army flew in supplies to Steinstücken. Later, American soldiers were stationed there as protection and accompanied the residents on their way to the city. In 1972 the Four-Power Accord provided Steinstücken with a street that accessed the western section directly. Naturally, the street was walled in on both sides.

The Eiskeller exclave in the northwest of Berlin was for years only accessible by cros-

Arbitrary checks. Lines of West Berlin cars waiting to enter East Berlin at the border crossing Bornholmer Strasse, Easter 1972

sing the border grounds through a fenced in corridor. West Berliners who had property there had to ring a bell at the border in order to gain entry.

There were other absurd situations at the inner-city border as well. For example in Kreuzberg (West Berlin) in 1986, where a Turkish man and his wife claimed a piece of no man's land that bordered directly on the Wall. Osman Kalin planted vegetables in the fallow area in front of the Wall. GDR patrols initially forbid the owner from taking possession of GDR property because legally the small garden was situated on East Berlin territory. Kalin didn't allow himself to be inti-

midated and continued to tend to his plot of land. The GDR regime finally left him alone.

The East Germans guarding the Wall also had to contend with people from the west side who attempted to cross the border. "Wall jumpers" they were called. These were people who refused to accept the Wall as a normal part of daily life and who engaged in intentionally provocative behavior at the Wall.

One of the most famous of these "Wall violators" was the American John Runnings. On a number of occasions in 1986–87, he attempted to illegally cross the border as an act of protest against the Wall. In the summer of 1986 he climbed the wall with a ladder and

balanced himself on the wall coping for 500 meters. GDR officials arrested him during one of these episodes and sent him back to the West, but a few days later he was undertaking a new attempt. This time he climbed onto the wall coping and pounded it with a hammer.

In 1988 a "mass flight" from the West to the East took place. A foolish political prank. Hundreds of demonstrators took over the so-called "Lenné Triangle" in an act of protest against the government's plan to build an Autobahn tunnel through the West Berlin Tiergarten park. The area, which today lies next to the Sony Center, was at the time part of the GDR, but it was situated beyond the Wall and merely enclosed by a metal fence. The West Berlin Senate needed this area to realize its tunnel plans and had made an agreement with the East Berlin government to acquire it on July 1, 1988. The West Berlin police surrounded the area for days, but could only watch idly as the squatters demonstrated. When the day of the property exchange arrived, there was only one route of escape open to protesters and that was over the Wall. Hundreds scaled the Wall and were taken into friendly custody by the People's Police. With the help of the East German authorities, the "refugees" reentered the West unbeknownst to the West Berlin police.

There was also a tragic side to the gray concrete structure on the west side. A number of people in the West took their lives like a Kamikaze pilot by ramming their cars at high speed against the solid concrete barrier.

Globetrotter S-Bahn. Transit train from East to West over the Humboldt Harbor, in the background the Reichstag

Sightseeing highlight: Wall grounds at Potsdamer Platz (1987)

The Wall ran through every obstacle (Neukölln 1981)

Wall Art . . .

The GDR government tried painstakingly to present a positive image abroad. The inhuman border grounds in the middle of Berlin were supposed to present as "clean" or even innocent an impression as possible – a ludicrous undertaking given the aggressive construction and its murderous function. But this didn't matter to the SED. Important was that the concrete wall facing the West appear as neutral as possible. Like the wall of a factory. Not particularly stylish, but necessary.

And so the concrete was covered over with hectoliters of white paint. Border soldiers worked exhaustively to paint over political slogans against the socialist system or against the division of the city that had been boldly scrawled onto the concrete. A huge white surface cut through rebellious West Berlin. What an enticement for creative minds – the largest canvas in the world right in front of their noses!

Freedom of expression. The rich diversity of free ideas just happened to find expression right here on the west side of the Anti-Fascist Protective Wall. The many kilometer long Wall was painted and sprayed from top to bottom in the 1980s. Both by famous and unknown artists, by professionals and amateurs. The GDR border regime discovered just how subversive artistic freedom can be.

Suddenly West Berlin delighted in its "colorful wall" of murals, graffiti and fantasy pictures. West Berliners enjoyed taking walks along the illegal art scene. The bright surface made the ugly border disappear from the cityscape.

The authoritarian state was of course intolerant of this anarchistic brushwork. And painted over it. And over it. Again and again. But the border guards lost their battle against the creative follies of the West. Or maybe they just ran out of paint.

The "Wall Artists" took advantage of the fact that the gray concrete monstrosity was – according to the law – mostly on eastern territory. Law enforcers from the West were therefore not in a position to put a stop to border violations. If they had even wanted to.

The graffiti star Thierry Noir painted his famous broad abstract figures on the Wall, undisturbed. He let his creative juices go wild from Potsdamer Platz all the way to the Schilling Bridge.

Kiddy Citny, another well-known artist, was also immortalized through his Wall paintings.

Just when the Wall Art had moved beyond subculture, and was receiving international recognition, the never-ending canvas disappeared.

With the fall of the Wall, its artists were granted the unexpected honor of having their works sold and put up for auction – just like a conventional work of art.

In June 1990, 75 colorfully painted pieces of the Wall were auctioned in Monte Carlo and went for 1.8 million German marks. Works by Thierry Noir and Kiddy Citny were acquired by the queen of cognac, Ljiljiana Hennesy, and the publisher's widow, Jaguba Rizzoli.

And so the work of a rigid power ended up as an admired and popular collector's item. Scattered over the four corners of the earth ...

Berlin's largest canvas was decorated by many different artists. Thierry Noir and Kiddy Citny painted and sprayed their motifs on the Wall in the eighties

The Fall of the Wall . . . November 9, 1989

A misunderstanding was born and it caused an avalanche. The false information spread like wild fire and the rumor became the truth. This was not how the SED leadership had envisioned the new GDR travel law: Masses of people storming the Berlin border-crossings in the middle of the cold night, cheering, celebrating, disrespectfully dancing on the Wall and turning the Anti-Fascist Protective Wall into a farce. The western media, eager for sensational news, interpreted – over-interpreted – the information provided by the SED politburo member, Günter Schabowski, and thus raised the expectations of people both in East and West Berlin. Even the GDR state television news program "Aktuelle Kamera," announced, just shortly after 7:30 p.m. on November 9, that "all GDR citizens may, on short notice and without giving any special reason, take personal trips out of the country."

In November 1989, the GDR leadership no longer held the reins of history. Back on August 13, 1961, the communist state leadership had taken its residents by surprise. Twenty eight years later, on the night of November 9, the population caught its rulers and their henchmen off guard. Long and arduous travel requests, complicated bureaucratic procedures? A new faith in the cursed authority? The citizens of the GDR had run out of patience. They were running the show now. On the streets, at demonstrations, in their demands for democracy and the right of travel. For weeks they had pushed the SED around, and now that the Socialist Unity Party was up against the wall, the people cheerfully leaped over it. It was the most peaceful revolution in Germany's history.

No-one could have predicted in 1989 that the conflict in the GDR would end without bloodshed. The old cadres of the SED party, especially the head of state, Erich Honecker, remained stubborn. "Neither an ox nor a donkey can stop the course of Socialism," was the aging Honecker's answer to the increasing calls for change. In an arrogant de-

The end of an era of fear and repression. The Wall in Dreilinden in front of memorial with Soviet tank (1990)

nial of its own situation, the East Berlin government refused to engage in reform efforts like those being taken in Moscow, Warsaw and Budapest. And while the "socialist brother-nations," Hungary and Poland, were taking steps towards a multiparty system and market economy, the GDR leadership in 1989 was having to contend with a new and unexpected mass migration. Once again "flight from the East" determined Germany's fate. But how was it possible for exodus to occur with the Wall in place and border surveillance perfected?

It was the disintegrating loyalty of the Warsaw Pact states that broke the back of the communist part of Germany. While the GDR was standing guard at the Berlin Wall, the Hungarians simply cut through the barbed wire at the border to Austria on May 2, 1989. There were holes now in the Iron Curtain that hung between the East and West. All at once, the usual summer vacation to Hungary became an opportunity for GDR citizens to take off for the West.

And that is exactly what happened. They

left in the thousands. On August 19 in Sopron, for instance, more people escaped from the GDR than ever before since the Wall had been built. On the fringe of a political event, more than 600 people triumphantly trampled across the border to Austria. At the same time, GDR citizens occupied the embassies of the Federal Republic in Prague and Budapest to try and force their emigration. On September 1, the dam finally broke. The Hungarian government – without consulting their partners – officially declared the border to Austria open. By the end of September, more than 25,000 GDR citizens had taken this route to enter the Federal Republic.

Following negotiations with Bonn, East Berlin permitted the embassy squatters in Prague and Warsaw to leave. "Letting off steam," went the SED strategy. It was their hope that when all those who wanted to emigrate were finally gone, peace would be restored to the state. They hoped in vain. Public pressure at home was increasing as well. The GDR government, which was preparing to celebrate the 40th anniversary of the Republic, was in a jam. Its citizens were out on the streets expressing with growing

A picture that traveled the world. Masses of people on top of the Wall in front of the Brandenburg Gate on November 10, 1989

self-confidence their dissatisfaction with the politics and economy of the socialist state. By mid September, the legendary "Monday demonstrations" had begun in Leipzig and intrepid citizens were on the streets calling for social change. First thousands came, then tens of thousands. Other cities followed: Erfurt, Zwickau, Magdeburg and Dresden. The entire GDR was in turmoil. Tensions between Moscow and the GDR were simmering over the Kremlin's fear that the SED might use force to repress the swelling resistance. When Mikhael Gorbachev, the general secretary of the communist party in the Soviet Union, visited East Berlin on October 7 for the celebration of the republic's 40th anniversary, he articulated his displeasure to the press in no uncertain terms: "Latecomers will be punished for life," he explained. All at once the GDR leadership was isolated in its own political camp.

Following the final state-ordained celebration, events happened in quick succession. On October 18, the head of the SED, Erich Honecker, resigns from all his party and state offices. Egon Krenz becomes his successor. On November 4, almost a half a million people in East Berlin transform the GDR state theater into a free theater of the people. They gather at Alexanderplatz, at the largest demonstration in the history of the GDR, and demand democracy, free elections and the freedom to travel. The socialist party under Krenz's leadership tries to set off on the right foot, but ends up reacting frantically and on November 7, the entire government of the GDR resigns. The next day, the old political elite is sent into retirement and the central committee of the SED elects a new politburo.

In this nervous atmosphere, in which the power of the state is visibly eroding, an international press conference is held on the evening of November 9. This is a new, unfamiliar gesture of openness. Günter Schabowski, member of the politburo and party spokesman, looks tired and overtaxed as he speaks before the many microphones and cameras of the international press. He is unaware of the content of the paper that Egon Krenz has just handed him to read.

At 6:53 p.m. he raises the sheet and reads the text out loud, fleetingly, haltingly, almost in a mumble: The SED leaders have agreed upon a new arrangement to "regulate the permanent emigration, that is to say, leaving the republic." GDR citizens may request personal trips without having to meet the requirements that have been necessary in the past. Approval will be given on short notice.

The journalists listen in astonishment and confusion. "Does this apply to West Berlin as well?" they ask.

Schabowski is at a loss, he fumbles in his papers. "Well (pause) – yes, yes." And he adds: "Exiting the country can proceed at all GDR border crossings to the BRD, or to West Berlin." "When does this take effect?"

Again he has no answer and stops short. "To my knowledge, it is to take effect immediately, without delay."

That was not in line with the resolution. The SED leadership had intended to contain the stream of refugees leaving the country by introducing a drawn out many week long application process for obtaining a GDR pass-port. An uninformed Schabowski had signed the states' death warrant. The misunderstanding was born and the West German media publicized the sensational news. GDR citizens were also watching "Tagesschau," the West German television news, at 8 p.m. when the top story ran: "The GDR opens the border!"

Berlin, Bornholmer Strasse border crossing. People begin arriving on the East Berlin side around 8:30 p.m. to test the "new travel freedom." Some demand that the border guards let them through, others have just come to see what's happening. The border guards are completely at a loss and have no idea what is in store for them. There are no orders, no information. The ministries are also unable to provide any explanations. The crowd is growing with every minute. It pushes towards the barrier, towards freedom. Loud demands to open the border can be heard. Cars are already piling up on Bornholmer Strasse. The checkpoints at Invalidenstrasse and Sonnenallee also report an onslaught. There is no point in waiting and trying to put off the people any longer. As the

---

Erich Honecker *(GDR chairman of the Council of State), on January 19, 1989*

Without the active cooperation of the GDR, without its willingness to seek compromise and to mediate, the Vienna meeting [CSCU] would not have reached a successful conclusion, especially not, if one considers how loudly some speak of human rights, while trampling them in their home countries. (…)

Which is why it is for example inexplicable that the USA – perhaps to reassure its allies – should lament the security facilities on the GDR border to Berlin (West), thereby disturbing the conclusion of the Vienna conference, assisted by Mr. Genscher and a few others, but deliberately overlooking the electronic barrier devices that are erected on the boundary between the USA and Mexico. (…)

The construction of the Anti-Fascist Protective Wall in 1961 stabilized the situation in Europe and peace was rescued. The reports today in some of the media of the FRG and West Berlin over "Vienna and the Wall" indicate not only short-sightedness, but also reveal the hypocrisy of politics in Bonn and Berlin (West). The

gentlemen from the Springer Press and those who assist them, appear to have forgotten that a permanent task of the government of a state should be to protect its citizens from plunder. (…)

So much can be said for now: irregardless of the "powerful performances" of Mr. Genscher and Mr. Shultz, the Wall will remain as long as the conditions that led to its erection remain unchanged. It will still exist in 50 and in 100 years if the existing reasons for it are not eliminated. (…)

That is necessary to protect our republic from thieves, not to mention from those who are willing to destroy the stability and peace in Europe. Securing the border is the sovereign right of every state, of our GDR, too.

situation intensifies, First Lieutenant Jäger, head checkpoint supervisor on duty at Bornholmer Strasse, demands rules of conduct from the State Security Service. A few people are quietly expatriated and permitted to leave the country. On their way out their papers are stamped invalid.

But the pressure doesn't stop. Just the opposite. "Open the gate! Open the gate!" the crowd vigorously demands. Jäger is worried that the people are going to storm the border guards and he begins to fear for the life of his subordinates. At 10:30 p.m. he calls off the security. "We are going to flood now!" he informs his supervisors and acting on his own authority, he raises the barrier.

The moment that for years had been longed for had finally come. The Wall falls. Thousands of people pour over the bridge to West Berlin. A little later the barriers at the Sonnenallee and Invalidenstrasse border-

sun is shining once again, but nothing is as it used to be. Many people, oblivious to the events of the night before, turn on their televisions to see hundreds of joyous people on top of the Wall at the Brandenburg Gate. They are celebrating the fall of the Wall. Twenty-eight years after the Wall was erected, the nightmare has ended. And a dream has come true. Berlin is again in an extreme situation. The entire city is intoxicated. The visitors from the GDR don't slow down for a moment. The city is submerged in a cheerful chaos. For weeks the Wall remains firmly in the hands of euphoric crowds. Although they have joined forces, the police from both East and West have difficulty preventing the boisterous individuals from destroying the concrete wall. Scenes take place that a few days earlier would not have been conceivable. On November 12, 1989, when the first official new border-crossing is opened at

Little Wall-pecker at Potsdamer Platz with a GDR border soldier (1990)

Resolution of the GDR Council of Ministers on the opening of the border-crossings, *November 9, 1989*

As was announced by the government speaker, the Council of Ministers of the GDR has resolved that until the People's Chamber arrives at a corresponding legal arrangement, the following measures for private travel and permanent emigration from the GDR to other countries shall come into effect immediately:

Applications for travel out of the country can be made without providing previously required information (reason for travel and relationship to relatives). Approvals will be issued without delay. Refusals will be issued only in exceptional

cases. The People's Police district office departments in charge of passports and registration in the GDR have been instructed to issue visas for permanent emigration without delay and without the presentation of prerequisites for a permanent emigration. Applying for permanent emigration is still possible at the Department for Internal Affairs. Permanent emigration can occur at all GDR border-crossing points to the FRG or Berlin (West).

With this resolution, the temporary approvals issued by the foreign representation offices [embassies] of the GDR and the permanent emigration with the GDR identification card via third states, will cease.

---

crossings are also opened and by midnight even Checkpoint Charlie is open. The people crossing the white border line are overwhelmed. They cry, cheer, and repeatedly shout in disbelief: "Crazy!" They are greeted on the west side by West Berliners. The entire night is a huge celebration, with champagne and total strangers befriending each other. An unforgettable night.

No-one is sticking to any rules. Even at Brandenburg Gate a number of people can be seen scaling the low part of the Wall from the west side at 11:30 p.m. The border soldiers use water hoses to stop them. But then even they capitulate and give in to the people's desire for freedom. Now even East Berliners are passing the border barrier and heading towards the Gate.

The next morning Berlin awakes and the

Potsdamer Platz, the GDR border policeman greets federal president Richard von Weizsäcker with the words: "Mr. President: no unusual incidents to report!"

On December 22, the Brandenburg Gate is finally opened.

And the Wall? Following the freedom-seekers' victory, it literally turns to dust. People begin chiseling away at the concrete. As the politicians of both German states prepare reunification, the structure ceases to inspire terror. Pieces of the Wall become popular souvenirs and mementos. Border checks are conducted "pro forma." On June 26, 1990, the GDR minister for disarmament and defense, Rainer Eppelmann, calls off the border checks at the inner-German border and in Berlin. In September, two weeks before German Unity, the border troops are disban-

ded and transferred to the Bundeswehr (Federal Army).

The former guards have long been busy destroying their worksites one by one. On Bernauer Strasse, at the corner of Ackerstrasse, the planned demolition of the border begins on June 13, 1990 under the direction of the Border Commando of Mitte with specialists of the People's Army and West Berlin companies. With massive machinery, about 106 kilometers of concrete is arduously removed. On November 30, 1990, the inner-city border has disappeared (with the exception of three commemorative pieces). Almost all the street connections are restored. The dismounted concrete segments, if they were not declared works of art, are shredded and used as the bottom layer of street construction in East Germany.

Willy Brandt *(former mayor of Berlin), November 10, 1989 in front of the Schöneberg city hall*

Dear Berliners, dear countrymen on both sides!

This is a great day after a long journey. But we are still at a way station. We have not yet reached the end of the journey. There is still much ahead of us.

The common bond between Berliners and Germans manifests itself in a moving and turbulent way, and is most moving where separated families are finally and unexpectedly reunited with tears in their eyes. I was moved by the picture of the policeman on our side who went over to his colleague and said: We have watched each other from a distance for so many weeks, maybe even months. I would like to shake your hand just once. That is the right way to address the situation. Shake hands, hold a grudge only when absolutely necessary. And, whenever possible, put your bitterness behind you. I also felt that this afternoon at the Brandenburg Gate. (…)

Everything now depends on whether we Germans, here and on the other side, are up to the challenge of the historical situation. That Germans come together, that is the issue. Coming closer together occurs differently than most people expected. And nobody should now act as if he knew exactly what form the new relationship between the people in both states would take. That they will enter into a new relationship, that they are free and can evolve as individuals, that is the important thing. It is clear that nothing in the other part of Germany will ever again be the way it once was. The winds of change that blew over Europe re-

cently didn't just pass over Germany. I was always convinced that the concrete partition and the division by barbed wire and death strip went against the current of history. And this summer I had put it down on paper once again. Berlin will live and the Wall will fall. By the way, dear friends, if it is up to me, we could let a piece of this terrible structure remain as a reminder of this historical monstrosity. (…)

Once again: It will never again be the way it was. This also means that we in the West will not be judged based on more or less pretty slogans of yesterday, but instead on what we do today and tomorrow, what we are willing and able to achieve, intellectually and materially. I hope that the intellectual reserves are not spent. I also hope that the cash box has more to hand out. And I hope that the appointment calendars have reserved space for that which now has to be. Willingness not to point the finger but to show solidarity, to even things out, to begin anew, that is what is being put to the test. This is the time to come together. Keep our heads clear and to do as well as possible what is in line with both our German interests and our duty to Europe.

Contemporary Witness . . . Eckard Löhde

November 9: Escalation of events. With every new hour, there is new information. The news is interesting. Berlin is suddenly at the center of the world.

Shortly before 7:00 p.m. there is a press conference in East Berlin. Questions, questions, rumors: the border is open? "Yes, just got this information in." When? "It says right here …" The countdown begins. I am still working at my desk. Every hour, every half hour, news. And then it really happens: They're coming over!

It is about 11:00 p.m. I go over to my housemate, Mark. We want to go to the border.

What a moment! Everywhere along the way West Berliners are greeting East Berliners. We first head towards the Brandenburg Gate. Traffic jam. People, lots of people – but it is still manageable. To the left, over to Invalidenstrasse. To the border-crossing. Cars parked illegally all over the place.

The border-crossing doesn't really exist anymore. A cluster of people fills the concrete narrow passageway between East and West. Spotlights.

Cheers. People really are coming from over there. Small colorful Trabis are sprayed with champagne. They look out – composed faces, or hidden behind hands, pale and tired, no heroes and yet suddenly in the glistening limelight, endlessly photographed. Most of them are not really photogenic enough for western drama. They hold back their tears. They wave, shake hands, and start from the constant banging on the roof of their Trabis. They are uncertain whether the car can stand it.

Only a few actually let their joyful feelings show. They shriek with delight and raise their arms. Everyone wants to touch them. The greeters express their joy more openly than the people being greeted.

The crowd on the west side is now also pushing forward. Inch by inch. It shouts: "The Wall must go!" We spur each other on. Every Trabi is a catalyst for more cheers. Meanwhile the large concrete barrier is overfilled with people. The first among us jump from the anti-tank obstacle to the East.

"Let us in! Let us in!" The joking becomes more meaningful. Four chubby border officials push the people back, friendly and strangely uncertain. Their faces reveal bewilderment and a little fear. Four against two hundred – it is absurd for us not to cross the border. But we "westerners" are uncertain, we don't want a fight. But a few do push forward, cautiously assessing the border guards.

I venture to take a deep step into the East. The Vopo repels my advance. "Okay, okay, just one second," I reply. "Just one photo of the entire crowd. Otherwise I can't get them all in the picture…" Meters have been gained, others move in from behind. Three steps forward, one step back. The crowd is starting to tremble, from the tension. Step by step. Step by step. I feel it clearly: We can take off with the next Trabi that crosses the border, we must take off! Mark and I are at the very front. "Let us in! Let us in!"

The Vopos are not able to keep the crowd under control any longer. You can feel that the border doesn't exist anymore. It is a street again, slightly strange , but nothing more. No more fear. Bulwarks turn into viewing platforms. And here it comes, the next Trabi, small, blue, on thin fragile wheels. It doesn't know what it is about to set off.

The knot busts, we take off. We run over the border grounds towards the East. Cold light, cold fence. No one stops us. We are on the other side.

"To Alex, to Alex. Where is it? Which way? Or even better, to the Brandenburg Gate. Straight ahead!"

We reach Unter den Linden. While we are waiting for the others we notice that we westerners are totally by ourselves here. Everything is empty and dark. No GDR residents in sight. We don't find anyone to address our enthusiasm to.

We continue. And there it is: The Brandenburg Gate.

Broader paces, the shouts become louder again. We are very excited. It is getting closer and closer. "The Wall is gone! The Wall is gone!"

The Gate towers before us. Large and impressive. Submerged in a warm light. The full moon shines conciliatory above. Silence. Full of historical power. The gate to freedom. I will never forget this picture under the low hanging moon. Just how many yearnings accompanied this view from the East?!

We reach the first obstacle on the large plaza in front of the gate. Four soldiers stand at the square. They don't take much notice of us. Suddenly we ask ourselves what we are doing here. Have we gone too far? We are in East Berlin, in the capital of the GDR: In front of us stands the most heavily guarded gate in the world. No-one else around for miles, an unusual quietness. No easterners to be found. Just us. Is it really true? Is the border really open? Or maybe it is closed again? I am overwhelmed by a sense of legal certainty. What could possibly happen to me, I wonder. I don't know what it is like to fear an unrestrained power. But still we all hesitate.

The first ones climb over the barrier. A few have difficulty and are slow to climb the 110 centimeter high fence. A few want to discuss it first and feel we have gone far enough. But those of us in front are getting louder: "Come on, let's go!" We reach a second barrier. And we're over it. We look around. Fortunately the others are following behind.

"The Wall is gone." Now, we run...

We jump, run, shout. The feeling is overwhelming. Running over this plaza, to the Brandenburg Gate. Let's go west!"

All of a sudden about fifty soldiers appear out of nowhere and are running towards us. In no time at all they have formed a massive human barrier with linked arms. We bounce back, shocked by our own courage.

What a picture. a colorful mix of westerners, howling with raised fists, a silent human barrier of armed border officials in uniform. The Brandenburg Gate looms larger under the moon ... and suddenly cold feet. Tense moments.

The others are pushing from behind. Apparently with all the excitement they haven't noticed the barrier. We run on, around both sides of the chain of soldiers – to the left and to the right. The men stand motionless. It is just a few more meters to the Brandenburg Gate.

The soldiers must have been totally surprised to see us there. In the prohibited zone. The plaza in front of the Brandenburg Gate and the gate itself were still a total taboo. An East Berliner would never have dared to climb over the barrier and run towards the gate, to enter this area.

While running through the Brandenburg Gate I am seized with the feeling that I am part of an historical moment. Not until now do I see the masses of people standing on the Wall facing the West. They cheer us because they think we are from the East.

And I feel an unexpected coldness. And then a stream of water hits me. People's Policemen are hunting us down, the border violators, with water hoses. Their last remaining weapon. They spray passionately, even aim at the people on the Wall. But then at some point they give up. They bow to history and the soldiers remove their helmets. This is the moment that people come down from the Wall, they fill up the cordoned off plaza, they speak with the border guards, share a smoke. It feels like a festival.

Mark and I retrace our steps along Unter den Linden to Alexanderplatz. It is a touch more lively by now.

We meet two young women in their early twenties. We greet them hoarsely and offer what is by now the somewhat worn out news of the evening: "The Wall is gone!" They both look totally stunned. "The Wall is gone?," the young girls ask in disbelief. They haven't heard anything about it. They just came from a discotheque. And suddenly it bursts out of one of the women. "Here take the house key. Say hi to mother. I am not going back. I am going with you right now. Grandma lives over there. Are we really allowed over – at the Brandenburg Gate?" We are astonished by her reaction. "I am not sure, to the West? Here, take my cigarettes, too. ID – do I need that? Can I really go over there? God, I am so excited. I was planning to leave over Czechoslovakia. I can first visit grandma. Bye, say hello to everyone from me. Is it really true? I can't believe it. I just can't believe it! And you guys are from the other side? That just can't be."

Taking long strides we head back again. "Yeah, sure, just over the Wall, snap, and you're over there." "But the soldiers?" "They just watch."

She is totally excited, but determined. Off to the other side!

The large plaza in front of the gate slowly comes into view. The young woman starts to quiet down. The conversation peters out. We climb over the first barrier. She says: "Oh my God!" Nothing else. By now there are a lot of people here. We climb over the second barrier. She cries. Mark takes her in his arms. She lets go of her tears now. She stumbles, cries, holds on tightly to Mark. We take her through the Brandenburg Gate, raise her up over the Wall. Lots and lots of hands reach out towards her, grab out to her hands, she's lifted up. Her eyes are wide open without appearing to see anything. She doesn't look back anymore. She climbs down the other side. British soldiers take care of her. Thank you, Thank you!

More and more people. We lose ourselves in the commotion. It definitely feels like a festival now at Brandenburg Gate. But I don't feel that way anymore. I go back to the car on Invalidenstrasse, along the Wall behind the Reichstag building. There are hardly any people here. It is quiet here. I see the memorial crosses adorned with flowers for the people who tried to get over the Wall at an earlier time. Many of the victims who died were the same age as the woman we accompanied to the West. How they must have been driven to attempt an escape! What in the world did they feel? Not one single hand had reached out to them from the Wall, not a single one. No one shouted :"Come on over, I'll help you!" No glistening and laughing eyes to embrace you.

doctor, has lived in Berlin (West) since 1986

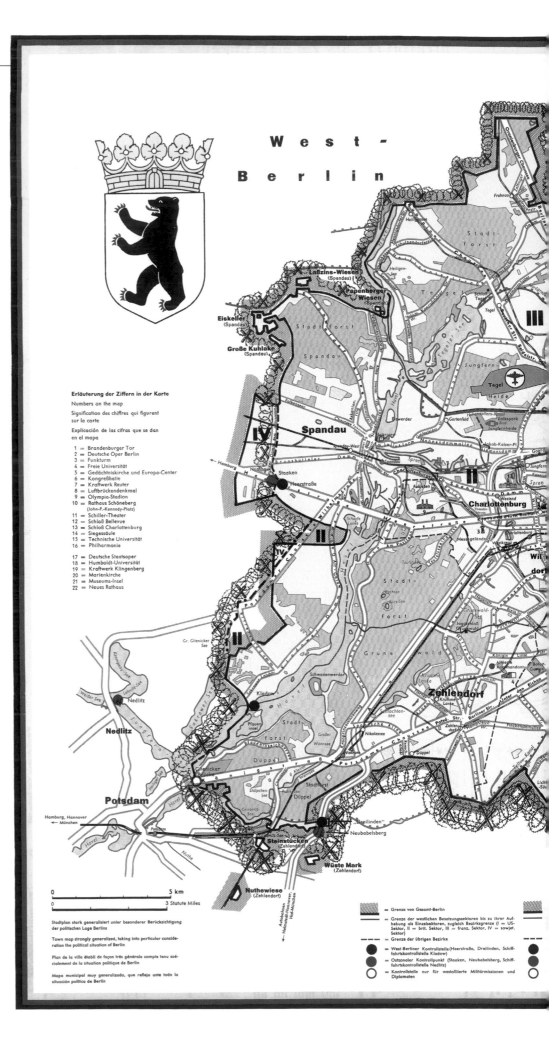

Erläuterung der Ziffern in der Karte

Numbers on the map

Signification des chiffres qui figurent
sur la carte

Explicación de las cifras que se dan
en el mapa

1 = Brandenburger Tor
2 = Deutsche Oper Berlin
3 = Funkturm
4 = Freie Universität
5 = Gedächtniskirche und Europa-Center
6 = Kongreßhalle
7 = Kraftwerk Reuter
8 = Luftbrückendenkmal
9 = Olympia-Stadion
10 = Rathaus Schöneberg
       (John-F.-Kennedy-Platz)
11 = Schiller-Theater
12 = Schloß Bellevue
13 = Schloß Charlottenburg
14 = Siegessäule
15 = Technische Universität
16 = Philharmonie

17 = Deutsche Staatsoper
18 = Humboldt-Universität
19 = Kraftwerk Klingenberg
20 = Marienkirche
21 = Museums-Insel
22 = Neues Rathaus

Stadtplan stark generalisiert unter besonderer Berücksichtigung
der politischen Lage Berlins

Town map strongly generalized, taking into particular conside-
ration the political situation of Berlin

Plan de la ville établi de façon très générale compte tenu spé-
cialement de la situation politique de Berlin

Mapa municipal muy generalizado, que refleja ante todo la
situación política de Berlin

December 24, 1989

West Berliners can once again visit the eastern part and the GDR without restrictions. Visa and compulsory money exchange for West Berliners is no longer required.

December 27, 1989

A company takes over the sale of Wall segments.

December 31, 1989

Half a million people celebrate New Year's Eve at the Brandenburg Gate.

April 12, 1990

The first freely elected government of the GDR under the leadership of minister president Lothar de Maizière takes office.

May 5, 1990

The Two plus Four talks to discuss foreign policy aspects of reunification begin in Bonn, attended by foreign ministers from the USA, Great Britain, France and the Soviet Union, and the two German states.

June 12, 1990

The first joint meeting of the West Berlin Senate and the East Berlin municipal government takes place.

June 30, 1990

The GDR border regime comes to an end.

July 1, 1990

The currency and social union is established.

October 3, 1990

Germany is reunified.

September 8, 1994

Germany bids farewell to its allies with a grand tattoo at the Brandenburg Gate.

The reunification celebration took place outside the Reichstag on the evening of October 3, 1990

Checkpoint Charlie

Creative escape vehicle in House at Checkpoint Charlie

The former Checkpoint Charlie border-crossing is an attraction for tourists from all over the world. The still enchanting site at Friedrichstrasse includes the guard house of the US Army, an original warning sign ("You are leaving the American Sector"), and above all, the oldest Wall Museum that the city has to offer. The "House at Checkpoint Charlie" was established at this focal point of the East-West conflict in 1963 to continuously make the public aware of the consequences of the divided city, of the persecution, escapes and inhuman occurrences at the border. This museum, which is overflowing with material from and about the Wall, is privately-run.

The exhibition focuses on the daring escapes and events that made border-history and it documents the sheer variety of ideas that GDR citizens had to escape into the free West. Visitors can see the basket of a self-made hot-air balloon that was used by two families from the GDR to flee to the Federal Republic in 1979; a mini U-boot with which people successfully escaped over the Baltic Sea; and two surfboards that enabled a young

woman to leave. But this amusing escape paraphernalia does not overlook the life-threatening situation in which these escapes attempts were made.

An authentic GDR spring gun in the museum reminds visitors of that danger. These kinds of deadly devices did not exist along the Berlin Wall, but mines and firing mechanisms that were set off by contact were installed along the inner-German border. This treacherous device was dangerously dismantled from the border.

Naturally, most of the Wall Museum is dedicated to the history of the Wall in Berlin, and specifically, to Checkpoint Charlie. It recounts, for example, a successful escape that was undertaken not far from the museum building: A family slid down from the building rooftop of what is now the Federal Ministry of Finance on Wilhelmstrasse. Unnoticed in the dark, the man, wife and child managed to sneak across the death strip that was especially narrow there without being detected.

Films on the history of the Wall accompany the exhibition. Commentaries are presented in four languages. Artistic objects relating to themes of division and resistance are displayed.

Next door to the "House at Checkpoint Charlie," the shop MES provides a very good selection of articles about Berlin (literature, illustrated books, postcards and much more). Wall souvenirs can also be purchased there.

> *Museum Checkpoint Charlie*
> *Open daily 9 a.m.–10 p.m.*
> *Friedrichstrasse 43–45*
> *U-Bahn station Kochstrasse*

Checkpoint Charlie as a tourist attraction. A guardhouse was rebuilt in 2001 for the day commemorating the building of the Wall

Wall Memorial

The Berlin Wall Memorial on Bernauer Strasse is the official site to commemorate the division of Berlin. The nearby Documentation Center, the Chapel of Reconciliation and the remains of the Berlin Wall make up an interesting ensemble that invites reflection.

The memorial site intentionally avoids presenting a spectacular scenario. The artistic monument, which was dedicated on August 13, 1998, addresses themes of separation and enclosure. A small section of the border strip, hermetically sealed off by two large panels of steel, has been left in the condition that it was found after the border was opened. An inconspicuous entrance on Ackerstrasse leads to what used to be the hinterland wall of the border strip. Visitors are only able to view the closed off security grounds by peering through slits in the cement slabs that make up the back wall. The memorial site, designed by the architects Kohlhoff & Kohlhoff, therefore, does not recreate the original border, but instead conserves the si-

The Chapel of Reconciliation on Bernauer Strasse

tuation as it was left after the Wall fell. This monument, which was highly controversial and hotly debated, emphatically conveys the atmosphere produced by an invincible, inhuman barrier. The monument's inscription reads: "In memory of the division of the city from August 13, 1961 to November 9, 1989 and to commemorate the victims of communist tyranny."

The Chapel of Reconciliation, a simple house of worship at Bernauer Strasse and Hussitenstrasse, also commemorates a chapter of Wall history. The neo-Gothic Reconciliation Church used to stand at the very same site with church steeple and entrance facing the Hussitenstrasse. After the Wall was built, the church remained for years caught in the middle of the border security grounds and unreachable to all its congregation members; most of them lived in the West. The church in the middle of the death strip and the figure of Jesus looming over the Wall was naturally a thorn in the side of the GDR regime. The Reconciliation congregation was forced to give up its church as part of a property exchange and the building was demolished on January 22, 1985. The church nave fell first, the tower a week later. According to the GDR State Security Service, the measure was necessary "to improve security and orderliness at the state border to West Berlin." The Reconciliation Chapel is a new place of worship on the site within the former death strip where the church had once stood. Designed by the architects Rudolf Reiterman and Peter Sassenroth, it is a simple construction in which a wooden foyer frames a small prayer room made of pounded clay. The bell and altar of the demolished church have

been returned to their original location, but the bells now hang in simple scaffolding outside of the chapel.

The Documentation Center at Bernauer Strasse 111 contains an exhibition with original GDR documents and a bookstore with publications about the building of the Wall and daily life with the Wall.

That memorialization is not for everyone is demonstrated by the strange break in the concrete wall next to the memorial site. The pastor of the Sophia Congregation, another church community in the area, on his own authority and in violation of historical preservation, had a piece of the border torn down. The property on which the Wall had stood belonged to the cemetery of his congregation.

A peek into the past at the Wall memorial

Memorial and Documentation Center
Tues. to Sun. 10 a.m.–5 p.m., April to Oct.
until 6 p.m.; admission is free
U-Bahn station Bernauer Strasse, S-Bahn station Nordbahnhof

The Wall as Big Seller

Berlin's longest structure refuses to die. Torn down long ago, broken into little pieces and recycled, it still continues to pop up at different places throughout Berlin and around the world.

Now that it has lost its evil function, the odious concrete monstrosity is popular and in demand as never before. The innovative uses for the notorious cement range from key ring to art object.

When the ca. 45,000 border segments ceased to spread terror, they became a popular collector's item. The individual and still intact segments with original Wall painting were, of course, especially desirable.

But by November 1989 such pieces were already difficult to come by. The people's scorn for the "Protective Wall" had taken its toll. The Wall was reduced to fragments with hammer and chisel and pieces were brought home as a personal trophy. The people who so feverishly worked to take down the border were nicknamed "Wall-peckers".

This spontaneous and anarchistic activity was soon exploited by commercial interest. Original pieces of the Wall were in high demand and sold like hotcakes. So the souvenir-sellers started hammering for all they were worth.

It is still possible to buy original pieces of the Wall today. As an accessory to a postcard, as a paperweight, key ring or hanging clock. These souvenirs are produced from real pieces of the Wall concrete at a storage lot north of Berlin.

Business is still good. The largest selection of Wall souvenirs is available at Checkpoint Charlie and the East-Side-Gallery.

Large selection of Wall souvenirs at MES at Checkpoint Charlie

After the fall of the Wall, the GDR realized the functionless border was a money-maker and it became the first large capitalist private enterprise of the socialist state. A company was commissioned to sell the still intact pieces of concrete for a good cause. And they were donated to national and international institutions. And so pieces of the Wall can now be found all over the World:

In front of German schools in Mexico City, in the cafeteria of Microsoft in Redmond/Washington, in front of the Janco-Dada Museum in the artist village Ein Hod in Israel, in the Vatican (painted by the artist Yadegar Azizi), in Cambridge, Massachusetts, in front of the NATO headquarters in Belgium and the German ministry of defense in Bonn, in

the parking lot of the CIA and the State Department in Washington, DC, in "Parque de Berlin" in Madrid.

And of course pieces of the Wall can be found in German cities and in Berlin (at Europa Center, for example). Ludwik Wasecki, a dentist from Poland, was particularly ecstatic about the world famous concrete. He purchased almost 50 Berlin Wall segments and grouped them as an outdoor artwork near Wrotzlaw. Most of his Wall pieces were painted by the graffiti artist Thierry Noir.

Stages of the Fall of Man. The Reconciliation Church on Bernauer Strasse is blown up on January 28, 1985

Reichstag and Brandenburg Gate

1 Wall Victims Memorial
2 Brandenburg Gate
3 Holocaust Memorial

The Brandenburg Gate with the Wall and a watchtower (1986)

After the Wall opened, the Berliners had only one wish: That the Wall that so brutally partitioned the city disappear at once. Places and neighborhoods that had been misused as border areas should be rebuilt.

The parliament quarter around the Reichstag and the Pariser Platz illustrate perfectly how Berlin pursued its heartfelt wish. A line of stone paved into the street where the Wall once stood is the only reminder of the division. The new buildings of the Bundestag purposefully connect the two city parts that had once been separated. The Reichstag building used to stand alone with its back to the Wall. The border ran along the east side of the German parliament building. The Spree river, too, had been part of the boundary. Today the parliamentarians work in office buildings that are situated directly on the former strip of the Wall. The Old Palace of the Reichstag president, today the residence of the Parliamentary Society, luckily survived the demolition craze of the East German government. The building next to the Reichstag used to stand on border territory and was often used as a listening post by the Stasi. The plaza between both buildings, today the entrance reserved for politicians, had once been the "death strip." Stone slabs of granite recall where the Wall once ran its course.

On the south side of the Reichstag building and on the bank of the Spree, white crosses commemorate the people who lost their lives at the Wall. On the other side of the Spree, next to the Bundestag library, a piece of art by Ben Wargin recalls the division: The "Parliament of Trees" was created from cement segments of the Wall.

When the Wall still stood, the Brandenburg Gate was a lonely symbol. Unreachable both from the East and the West, it stood tightly guarded within the grounds of the border. Only state visitors of the GDR were able to visit the historical city gates. From the west side, however, it was possible to come pretty close to the landmark. In the East the barriers stood far back at the Hotel Adlon. Pariser Platz was completely empty. Its present design was created after the Wall fell.

The Brandenburg Gate was always a political issue. After the war, the heavily damaged structure was rebuilt in a cooperative effort between East and West. The eagle and Iron Cross in the laurel wreath of the Goddess of Victory been removed by the leaders of the GDR. After unification, they were returned.

South of the Berlin landmark the "field of steles" (by Peter Eisenman in 2005) commemorates the victims of the Holocaust.

S-Bahn station Unter den Linden
Time: 20 Minutes

Memorial crosses for victims of the Wall at the Reichstag

From Potsdamer Platz to Niederkirchnerstrasse

The Potsdamer Platz, once the heart of Berlin, a world famous business district and pulsating traffic junction, was hurt the worst by the Wall. It was simply buried under walls, anti-tank obstacles and no man's land. And quite rigorously. Ruins in the eastern sector that were left from the war were torn down.

The Potsdam train station, Haus Vaterland, Haus Columbus and the Wertheim department store disappeared. The S-Bahn and U-Bahn stations were walled up. In the West, the only buildings that were spared during the reparceling of urban land were the Huth Weinhaus and the remains of the Grand Hotel Esplanade. A cosmopolitan city became a wasteland, a military no man's land in the middle of the city.

Although there was nothing to see there, busloads of tourists always headed for this lifeless area. Visitors looked in amazement at the huge expanse of the death strip. The GDR leaders had been able to destroy the architecture, but not the aura of the area.

It was therefore no surprise that three days after the Wall fell, on November 12, 1989, the GDR removed the first piece of the Wall from Potsdamer Platz and established a new border-crossing there. Starting then, life returned to the plaza. Today, next to the office tower of the Deutsche Bahn, right next to the entrance to the Potsdamer Platz train station, a piece of the Wall recalls this moment. Stone slabs in the ground indicate where the Wall once stood. Potsdamer Platz, once the intersection of the American, British and Soviet sectors, was also the site where on June 17, 1953, the conflict broke out between demonstrating GDR workers and Soviet tanks.

If you continue along the Stresemannstrasse to the south, you'll pass by five meters of colorfully painted Wall remains. They were part of the hinterland wall. A narrow street located behind the piece of Wall leads to a historically protected watchtower. When the Wall still stood, it was only possible to walk on the west side of the Stresemannstrasse sidewalk.

A very long piece of the Wall has been preserved on Niederkirchnerstrasse, which runs off Stresemannstrasse. This section of the Wall was heavily marred by "Wall-peckers," who after November 9, 1989 attacked the

border barrier with their tools. This wall, where today the exhibition "Topography of Terror" is displayed, was the border to the West. Two dark chapters of German history collide here: At an earlier time, the terror apparatus of the Third Reich, the Gestapo and SS headquarters, had been located on these grounds.

The huge building on the other end of the Wall is the seat of the Federal Ministry of Finance. In the GDR it had been the "House of Ministries" and after that, until 1994, it served as the office of the trust company for the privatization of East German businesses. This office complex was built by the Nazis as an Aviation Ministry.

The Berlin Parliament Building (Abgeordnetenhaus) used to be the Prussian State Parliament (Landtag). Although it stood within the border strip, the building survived the GDR because the German Communist Party was founded there in 1918–19.

S- and U-Bahn station Potsdamer Platz.
Time: 30 minutes

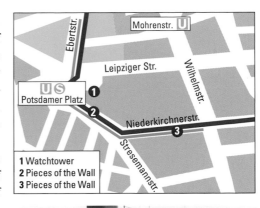

1 Watchtower
2 Pieces of the Wall
3 Pieces of the Wall

Repairing the Wall at Potsdamer Platz (1966)

Marveling at the remnants of the Wall near the Martin Gropius Building

Checkpoint Charlie

1 Wall Museum
2 Checkpoint Charlie
3 Peter Fechter Memorial

Checkpoint Charlie is known throughout the world and is one of Berlin's most popular sightseeing attractions. The former border-crossing between the American sector (Kreuzberg) and the Soviet sector (Mitte) split the Friedrichstrasse in two. The small, white

guardhouse of the US army that was rebuilt in 2001 for the 40th anniversary of the building of the Wall, recalls the episode that almost inflamed the Cold War. In October 1961, American and Soviet tanks stood at this intersection just a hundred meters apart in a face off.

The confrontation began on October 22, 1961 when the GDR flexed its muscle. At this crossing, which was only used by members of the Allies and foreigners, the GDR People's Policeman on duty demanded that the US envoy, Allan Lightner, show his ID before entering East Berlin. Lightner angrily refused since according to Berlin's four-power status, only the Soviet army had that authority. After the GDR border officers repeated this game on the following days, the

American general, Lucius C. Clay reacted with the means at his disposal – those of a world power: A number of American tanks moved into position on October 25 at 8:30 a.m. on the west side of Checkpoint Charlie. A battle of nerves and endurance began. On October 26 the Soviet sector called in their tanks. The situation became critical. The confrontation between both world powers could escalate into an armed conflict. The telephone lines between Washington and Moscow were buzzing.

After about 48 hours, the Soviet tanks withdrew. Shortly thereafter, the Americans cleared out their position. The GDR leadership had given in and Allied officers could once again enter East Berlin unchecked. Neither of the superpowers wanted a war

Soviet tanks on Friedrichstrasse on October 28, 1961

over Berlin. Khrushchev explained in short: "If the tanks moved forward, that meant war. If they moved back, that meant peace."

If you walk two blocks east along Zimmerstrasse, which was once the death strip, you'll come across the memorial for Peter Fechter. About a year after the Wall had been put up, on August 17, 1962, the 18-year-old bricklaye apprentice decided to flee with a friend to the West. They climbed over the fence outside the control strip and suddenly came under the fire of the border soldiers. Twenty-one bullets were shot in total. His friend managed to climb over the wall in the hail of bullets. Peter Fechter, shot in the stomach and back, laid with his serious wounds on the east side of the wall. No-one came to his assistance as he bled to death. Not the GDR border guards, nor the US soldiers on duty at Checkpoint Charlie. Fechter cried out for help but the policemen from West Berlin, on the other side, were unable to reach him and could merely throw gauze bandages to him over the wall. Hundreds of Berliners listened as the young boy's painful cries became fainter. After about an hour, the lifeless Fechter was carried away by the GDR border policemen. The bronze statue recalls Peter Fechter's agonizing death. He was the 31st fatal victim in the first year of the Wall's existence. Weeks earlier, on June 18, 1962, the border soldier Reinhold Huhm had been shot and killed by a refugee on the Zimmerstrasse.

U-Bahn station Kochstrasse or Stadtmitte
Time: 30 minutes

Checkpoint Charlie today with the old warning sign

Bethaniendamm and Engelbecken

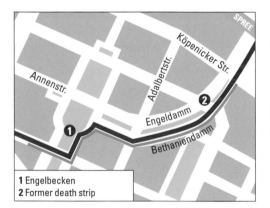

1 Engelbecken
2 Former death strip

This tour travels along the district border to Kreuzberg, the neighborhood with the highest population density in all Berlin.

The building of the Wall had serious consequences for this working-class district which was practically closed off by it on three sides. The district section called SO 36 became a dead end which led to its flourishing as a niche for counterculture.

The border to the Mitte district today, which then also functioned as the sector border, runs along Waldemarstrasse, at the corner of Leuschnerdamm.

The gardens in the middle of Leuschnerdamm and Legiendamm are worth taking a closer look at.

The green middle strip developed in 1926 along the route of the Luisenstadt Canal that had been filled up after it was no longer in use. The narrow park with imaginative garden ornamentation continued all the way to Köpenicker Strasse. On August 13, 1961, the recreational area was buried under the Wall and anti-tank obstacles.

The Wall bordered the sidewalk directly on Leuschnerdamm and around the bend to Bethaniendamm. The sidewalk actually belonged to the eastern sector. Only the houses stood on western territory. But as in other areas as well, here the GDR government had the barrier set a few meters behind the border line on eastern territory. As a result there was a narrow strip between the Wall and the western sector that was still under the jurisdiction of the GDR. Border troops used it to do maintenance work on the Wall or for patrolling. West Berliners also took over this piece of no man's land and planted gardens on it. This was prohibited by the GDR, but usually tolerated.

The Wall turned the Leuschnerdamm into a medieval-like street. All but the sidewalk remained off-limits to the western residents. Today they can once again enjoy the partially restored gardens. The 22 meter long "Engelbecken" (angel basin) is especially popular. A number of new buildings were erected on the east side of the grounds after the Wall came down.

U-Bahn station Kottbusser Tor
Time: 45 minutes

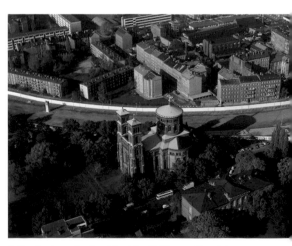

Bethaniendamm border strip at the St. Thomas Church in Kreuzberg (1988)

East-Side-Gallery

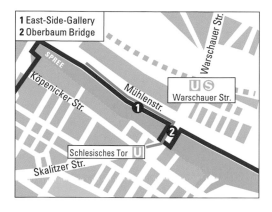

1 East-Side-Gallery
2 Oberbaum Bridge

Along Mühlenstrasse at the Ostbahnhof train station in Friedrichshain, East German residents had the rare "pleasure" of having a view of the border grounds, a privilege usually reserved for westerners. Because the Spree river made up the border here, the GDR government was compelled to erect the concrete wall to the west sector on its own river bank. After the SED regime collapsed, the East Berliners had the pleasure of painting the now purposeless wall the way the westerners had done for years. Over a hundred artists immortalized themselves along the 1.3 kilometer long wall. Some politically, others poetically, some ironically, others idealistically. The imaginative work of art captured the atmosphere of the time. The East-Side-Gallery has been placed under historical preservation.

If you start from the Ostbahnhof and walk along the East-Side-Gallery, you'll come to the Oberbaum Bridge. (A souvenir shop here sells Wall mementos). The neo-Romanesque structure is the longest of the historical bridges over the Spree in Berlin. The bridge used to be a border-crossing. That is why the subway line that runs over it to Warschauer Strasse was cut off when the Wall was built.

The entire breadth of the Spree belonged to the eastern sector. This had fatal consequences for a five-year-old boy who lived in the western part in 1975. Little Cetin from Kreuzberg was playing on the river bank when he fell into the Spree. After a few minutes West Berlin rescue service arrived, but the divers were not allowed into the water because it belonged to the heavily guarded border area. They were forced to helplessly watch as the young boy drowned. By the time the GDR border boat arrived at the scene of the accident, there was nothing else to do but pull the dead body of the young Turkish boy out of the water.

The tragic death led to an agreement between West and East Berlin which provided for mutual emergency assistance in the waters of the border area.

S-Bahn station Ostbahnhof, S- and U-Bahn station Warschauer Strasse
Time: 45 minutes

Artistic freedom against the concrete bulwark: the East-Side-Gallery at Mühlendamm

Invalidenstrasse

This Wall tour goes from border-crossing to border-crossing.

If you turn right at the former Chausseestrasse checkpoint you will come to Boyenstrasse, a quiet street that leads to the Spandauer Shipping Canal. This used to be the death strip. The street ends at the Bundeswehr hospital, which used to be part of the GDR government hospital before 1989. Continuing along Scharnhorststrasse, turn into the Kieler Strasse. Just before the canal, between two new residential buildings, you can see an original watchtower from the former Wall strip. The building, which is an historically protected monument, vividly conveys the threatening atmosphere at the inner-city border.

After the Wall fell, the strip of the border was transformed into an attractive river bank promenade. If you follow the promenade to the south you'll come to a sparse green area with a few scattered grave-stones. This is the Invaliden Cemetery (Scharnhorststrasse 25).

Half of this historically significant cemetery was recklessly leveled when the border was put up. These elaborate graves were destroyed and taken away so that a "fire and observation field" could be established. The SED regime did not have a problem with this desecration of culture and graves, especially since it was primarily officers and generals of the hated Prussian monarchy who were buried here. Three pieces of the Wall have been preserved on the grounds, including a 100 meter long hinterland wall that cuts straight through the cemetery over graves and burial sites. The renovated old cemetery

Remnants of the Wall at the Invaliden Cemetery

wall on the canal was used as a barrier to the West.

The canal promenade continues behind the Federal Ministry of the Economy. On the opposite side of the canal you can see the Hamburg Station Museum. In May 1962 GDR border guards and West Berlin police officers exchanged fire here. The conflict erupted because the border soldiers continued to recklessly shoot at a 15-year-old refugee, even after he had already reached the safe bank of the West. So the West Berlin police returned the fire. The 21-year-old border soldier, Peter Göring, was fatally injured. Most likely by a ricocheted bullet from his own troops.

The Sandkrug Bridge was built in 1994 where the Invalidenstrasse border-crossing used to be. On May 12, 1963, an unsuccessful escape with a van was attempted here. The van was unable to break through the wall. The 13 young passengers inside the bus were shot at, injured and imprisoned.

Traces of the border – walled up building entrance and barred windows – can still be found along Invalidenstrasse.

U-Bahn station Reinickendorfer Strasse,
S-Bahn station Hauptbahnhof
Time: 45 minutes

The watchtower between new buildings on Kieler Strasse

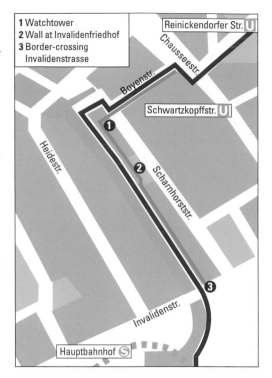

1 Watchtower
2 Wall at Invalidenfriedhof
3 Border-crossing Invalidenstrasse

Bernauer Strasse

House facade in front of Wall border, Bernauer Strasse (1979)

Nowhere in Berlin were the drastic consequences of the divided city presented to the world more clearly than at Bernauer Strasse. And nowhere can the absurdity of the division be more vividly felt today than at Bernauer Strasse. For one, because Berlin erected the Berlin Wall Memorial on the border grounds here.

If you arrive from the Nordbahnhof station, be aware that you are exiting into no man's land. The underground station, like 15 other stations, was for 28 years a "ghost station." Closed off and walled up because the West Berlin lines crossed East Berlin territory. From the Bernauer Strasse exit you practically step onto the area where the Wall once stood. And a short way from here stands the actual wall, about 80 meters of it, which was spared from demolition in the summer of 1990.

Before August 13, 1961, Bernauer Strasse was a normal residential street in a densely populated Berlin neighborhood. On both sides of the street there stood tenement houses, lined up one after the other. None of that remains today. It would have fateful consequences for Bernauer Strasse that the street belonged to West Berlin, but the houses on the south side were part of the east district of Mitte. The neighbors at Bernauer Strasse lived in different sectors. For the residents of buildings no. 1–50, this meant that after August 13, their windows facing Bernauer Strasse were the border to the GDR. As a matter of course when the border went up, the doors of these buildings were sealed – but not the windows. That came later. So hundreds of people began to flee through the windows. There were dramatic scenes and even deaths.

The builders of the Wall put a harsh stop to the "window jumps." In September the residents on the East Berlin side were forced to leave their apartments. The empty apart-

1 Wall Memorial
2 Documentation Center
3 Reconciliation Church
4 Tunnel 29
5 Mauerpark

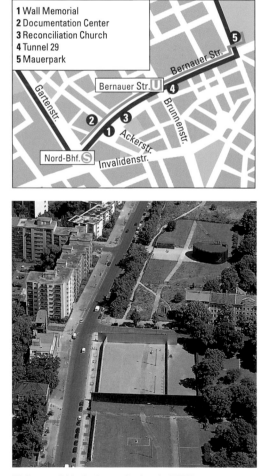

Wall memorial in the former death strip (2005)

ments were permanently walled up and later torn down. A broad, perfected border strip was put up in their place and can still be seen today in the middle of the residential area. In order to increase visibility across the grounds, the GDR blew a church up in 1985. (see "Wall Memorial")

When the above ground escape routes were blocked, people began to dig secret tunnels beneath the Bernauer Strasse. At the corner of Wolgaster Strasse, for example, 29 people escaped through the "Tunnel 29" (see Wall against the People). The largest escape tunnel was completed in 1964. It began in the basement of a shut down bakery. It ran twelve meters deep and 145 meters to the east. From October 3–5, 1964, 57 refugees crawled through the narrow passageway to the West. On the third night the tunnel was discovered by GDR border guards.

At the corner of Ackerstrasse is the Berlin Wall Memorial and Documentation Center (Bernauer Strasse 111). Since 2003 it also has a viewing platform which offers an excellent view of the border strip.

There are also a number of information panels along the street which describe events at the Wall. The tour ends at the Mauerpark (Wall park) on Eberswalder Strasse.

S-Bahn station Nordbahnhof,
U-Bahn station Bernauer Strasse
Time: 45 minutes

From the Mauerpark to Bornholmer Strasse

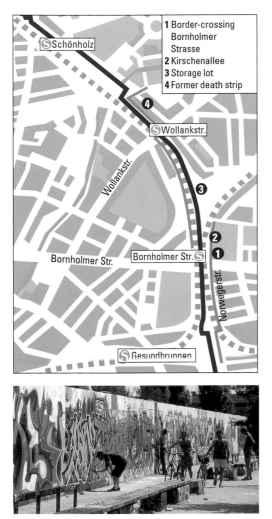

1 Border-crossing Bornholmer Strasse
2 Kirschenallee
3 Storage lot
4 Former death strip

Space for all kinds of graffiti: Wall remnants in the newly designed Mauerpark

The builders of the Wall had an easy time between Prenzlauer Berg and Wedding. Railroad tracks, embankment and railroad grounds already formed a "natural" barrier between the neighboring districts. The city of Berlin has plans to make the strip of the border between the new "Mauerpark" (Wall park) at Eberswalder Strasse and the old "Bürgerpark" in Pankow into a long recreational walking trail. The first step has already been achieved in the Mauerpark, where a piece of the old hinterland wall still stands on the hill. This popular park at Eberswalder and Schwedter Strasse was created after the city was reunified. The Schwedter Steg, a good five hundred meter long path over the railroad grounds, leads to Behmstrasse. Thirteen years after the fall of the Wall, the reconstruction of the Behmstrasse Bridge (1994–2001) again connects the districts of Prenzlauer Berg and Wedding. The bridge is one example of how costly restoring the city to its unified form can be for Berlin.

Beneath the Behmstrasse, continue along the Norwegerstrasse towards the Bösebrücke. The wall of the railroad grounds, by the way, also served as the border barrier. The Bornholmer Strasse border-crossing was located at the Bösebrücke. An inconspicuous commemorative stone recalls the momentous night of November 9, 1989. This is the first place where the Wall opened. On the north edge of the street there is still a piece of the old concrete wall from the border area.

If you leave Bornholmer Strasse again and go towards the garden colony, you can walk along a section of the former death strip. Today Japanese cherry trees align the old border troop patrol path. The walk ends for now at the Esplanade street.

It is worth taking a short trip with the S-Bahn along the former border grounds between Bornholmer Strasse and Wollankstrasse. The route along the border still operated when the city was divided. Just beyond Bornholmer Strasse there is a storage area situated between two railroad tracks. Beginning in 1990, the torn down pieces of the Wall were scrapped and shredded here. You can still find debris and Wall remains here. The Wollankstrasse train station was a one-of-a-kind. It was situated on eastern territory but used by the West. From the northern exit at Schulzestrasse you can reach the old border strip, situated between the railway embankment and residential build-ings. That is also where the cherry tree lane begins and continues all the way to the Bürgerpark.

The old border lampposts still exist in part along the grassy strip (but the covers are new). Old electricity boxes can also be found hidden behind overgrown shrubs.

U-Bahn station Eberswalder Strasse or Bernauer Strasse, S-Bahn station Bornholmer Strasse
Time: ca. 1 hour

Site of the historic border opening: The Böse Bridge on November 10, 1989

Contents

Documents and speeches:

press conference from Walter Ulbricht (June 15, 1961) 9, speech by Willy Brandt (August 16, 1961) 11, peech by John F. Kennedy (June 26, 1963) 18, speech by Ronald Reagan (June 12, 1987) 24, speech by Erich Honecker (January 19, 1989) 30, resolution on the opening of the border-crossings (November 9, 1989) 31, speech by Willy Brandt (November 10, 1989) 32

Contemporary witnesses:

Miriam Flotow 13, Heinz Knobloch 20, Joachim Rudolph 21, Eckhard Löhde 32

Imprint

3rd Edition 2005
© 2002–2005 Jaron Verlag GmbH, Berlin
(Original title: "Geteilte Stadt. Die Berliner Mauer")
All rights reserved. This publication must not be reproduced in whole or in part without the consent of the publisher. That especially applies to reproductions, translations, micro-film and storage and processing with electronic media.
Translation: Miriamne Fields, Berlin
Cover design: Atelier Kattner, Berlin, using photographs by Günter Schneider (Brandenburg Gate from West, 1986; Brandenburg Gate from East, 1987; Steinstücken 1990)
Text by Heinz Knobloch, p. 20, from: Heinz Knobloch, Stadtmitte umsteigen, Jaron Verlag 2002
Repro: alias of artificial and advertising gmbh, Berlin
Typography: Veronika Giesler, Berlin
Maps: Matthias Frach, Berlin; historic map from 1961: Presse- und Informationsamt des Landes Berlin
Printed and bound by: Druckhaus Köthen GmbH, Köthen
Printed in Germany
ISBN 3-89773-059-6
ISBN 3-89773-061-8 (10 copies)

Abbildungsnachweis:

Günter Schneider, Berlin: pp. 2, 3 bottom, 4, 17, 20, 23 top, 24, 26, 27, 29, 30, 31, 33, 38, 39, 40, 41, 42, 43 bottom, 44 top right, 44 bottom right, 45, 46, 47 left, 48 / Landesarchiv Berlin: pp. 7, 14, 15, 16 (except top left), 18, 19, 23 bottom, 25, 28, 32, 34 top, 47 right (Klaus Lehnartz); p. 5 bottom (Henry Ries); pp. 10, 16 top left (Horst Siegmann); pp. 5 top, 6, 8, 11, 12, 44 top left / Christian Bahr: p. 13 / Presse- und Informationsamt des Landes Berlin: p. 3
p.2: Spandau 1981; p. 3: Bernauer Strasse 1981, p. 48: East-Side-Gallery